Crossing the Rubicon

Ne Pleure Pas Si Tu M'aimes

"Don't cry if you love me"

Death is nothing. I only have passed to the other side. I am me. You are you. That which we were for each other, we are still. Give me the name you have always given me. Speak to me as you have always done. Don't use a different tone. Don't adopt a sad or solemn air. Continue to laugh at those things that made us laugh together. Pray, smile, think of me, pray with me. May my name be pronounced at home as it always has been, without emphasis of any kind, without the trace of a shadow. Life still means what it meant. It is that which has always been: the thread has not been cut. Why would I be out of your thoughts? Simply because I am out of your sight? I am not far, just on the other side of the path. You see, everything is fine. You will rediscover my heart, in it you will rediscover pure tenderness. Dry your tears and don't cry if you love me.

– St. Augustine, d.604, first archbishop of Canterbury

Animals are hearts wrapped in fur.

– Sister Michelle, beloved friend,
nun, and fellow chiropractor

To Erica
In friendship
and with love,

Juli

1.11.22

Crossing the Rubicon

Celebrating
the Human-Animal Bond
In Life and Death

Xenophon Publications
Cottage Grove, Wisconsin

CROSSING THE RUBICON

Celebrating the Human-Animal Bond In Life and Death

© 1999 by Julie A. Kaufman, D.C., C.A.C.

Front cover design and artwork by Kathy Esch

Book design by Raven Tree Arts

Published by Xenophon Publications
P.O. Box 21, Cottage Grove, WI 53527 USA 608-251-6303

Library of Congress Catalog Card Number: 99-90726

ISBN 0-9672085-0-5

Printed in the United States of America

DEDICATION

For
Mr. Spike and Pasha
who taught me
unconditional love
and
partnership

Bless all of the animals
who have given us
the gift of love and insight.
The connection
we share with you
relates us all
to all that is
in one common spirit.
Every birth
and every death
is shared by and belongs to all.

Table of Contents

FOREWORD i
Karen Dale Dustman

ACKNOWLEDGMENTS iii

PREFACE v
Dr. Julie Kaufman

INTRODUCTION
• How To Use This Book vii
• Relaxed Breathing and Tension Release vii

CHAPTER ONE: The Grief Wave
• Interview with Deborah Sullivan 3
• Brownie *by Terry LaMantia* 7
• Kate *by Laura Borman* 9
• Cissy and Megan *by Barbara Walsh* 13
• Phantoms *by Cheryl Sheehan* 17
• My Father's Dog *by Julie Kaufman* 19
• Workbook Exercise 23

CHAPTER TWO: Options
• Interview with Dr. Dawn Mogilevisky 27
• Connor *by Carmen Rasmussen* 39
• The Dog Who Loved Too Much *by Margaret Rowland* 41
• Frewin – My Free and Noble Friend *by Maia Michalson* . . . 43
• Frewin *by Sue Daubner* 47
• Time in the Tiger's Eye *by Julie Kaufman* 49
• Workbook Exercise 53

CHAPTER THREE: Letting Go
- Interview with Heather Evans 57
- The Odd Couple *by Bobby Mallace* 63
- Roscoe *by Rick Binder* 67
- I Lay You Down To Rest *by Mickey Hopper* 71
- Daydreamer *by Amy Crane Johnson* 73
- Picture of Cat *by Elizabeth Johnson* 75
- Thank Your Lucky Stars *by Julie Kaufman* 77
- Workbook Exercise 81

CHAPTER FOUR: Into the Light
- Interview with Adrienne Martin 85
- Bruiser, My Best Friend *by Sue Heilberger* 93
- Memories of Mitzi *by Kathy Agenten* 95
- The Super Dynamic One *by Synthia Smith* 99
- Thirteen Grams *by Amy Crane Johnson* 105
- For the Love of doG *by Julie Kaufman* 107
- Workbook Exercise 111

CHAPTER FIVE: In a Different Voice
- Interview with Asia Voight 115
- Blackie *by Dhani Mertin-Zovic* 131
- Misty *by Sue Aldene* 133
- Empathy of a Mare *by Amy Crane Johnson* 137
- Crossing Over *by C.O. Smith* 139
- Learning About Love *by Julie Kaufman* 143
- Workbook Exercise 151

Resources and Recommended Reading/Web Sites 153

Contributors' Notes 155

Foreward

It's hard to put words to the very special relationship we have with the animals in our lives. We call them our *animal companions*, but most of us know they're really more than that. They're our friends, our support system, our teachers, our healers. They share our lives, our tears, our beds, and sometimes even our illnesses.

Death is another of those concepts we Westerners often have a tough time talking about. But ask anyone who's lost a truly bonded animal friend, and they'll tell you it can be a painful and bewildering experience. Death, after all, seems so final. Like Caesar crossing the Rubicon, there's no turning back.

That's exactly where this book comes in – to give words to our feelings, and to *talk* about these things that we have such difficulty expressing.

If you're mourning a beloved animal companion, this is clearly a book of comfort. But read deeper, and I think you'll discover it is more than that. It's also a psalm of thanksgiving for the gift of love that animal companions bring to our lives. And it's a reminder that love transcends time, place – and even death.

Welcome to a very special book. May it touch your heart, as it has mine.

Karen Dale Dustman

Crossing the Rubicon

Acknowledgments

I would like to express my gratitude to all the clients, friends and professionals who gifted me with their stories and knowledge in order to help others bridge a difficult transition.

Many thanks to doctors' Thomas Truesdell, Maria Glinski, Tom Cameron, Dawn Mogilevsky, Bob Racich, Deb Schroeder, Sandy Sawchuck, Steve Frame, Laura Knipfer, Bob Magnus, and especially to my mentor Sharon Willoughby, for supporting my work early on when it was not yet accepted as a mainstream part of animal care. Their courage and foresight allowed the animal chiropractic profession to take hold and emerge as a viable treatment for many animals that would have otherwise suffered needlessly. I would also like to thank the staff members of Truesdell Animal Hospital and Silver Spring Animal Wellness Center, especially Barb Bachman and Karen Kjell, for their support over the years.

I want to thank Margaret Rowland for her patience and commitment throughout this entire project. Her gentle guidance contributed significantly to its completion. Thanks also to Cindy Binder for her enthusiasm and editing. Her "microscopic" analysis of the material really helped us in the final stages. My appreciation to Jan Harris for transcription work, friendship and support. Thanks also to Nikki Van Den Heuvel for her time and support. And my thanks to Ellen Bertram for her help with the guided meditation and relaxation technique.

Much thanks to Kathy Esch for her fabulous artwork and talented cover design. Her work illuminates an animal's inner soul.

And finally, many thanks to all the contributors.

Crossing the Rubicon

Preface

If you are reading this book you have probably just lost a pet. I want you to know that you are not alone. My hope for you is that you will find some support, peace, and healing within these pages.

The stories and poems were written by people who have experienced the death of a pet. They were graciously contributed with the intention of helping others find peace and healing during and following the loss of an animal.

In my animal chiropractic practice, I have seen how the loss of a pet invokes the same emotional response as the loss of a close friend or family member. It can be as devastating as the loss of a spouse or a child. The sense of emptiness, loneliness and depression following this loss takes time and supportive understanding to heal. These stories are intended to provide a sense of sharing to aid in the healing process.

This book was written as a gift of love to my clients, and also to fill a void that currently exists in literature. As I did research in the field of pet loss, it became apparent that there was a need for more focus in the area of such loss.

Please know that you are not alone in your pain. The loss of a pet can be one of the most devastating experiences of your life. My hope is that you can take the love you shared and creatively bring it forth into the world for others to experience in some unique way. May you find and foster the gift of the human-animal bond in such a way that it can be celebrated beyond death.

Crossing the Rubicon

Introduction

How To Use This Book

Each chapter contains poems, stories, interviews and exercises that may be read independently, or from cover to cover. They vary greatly in content and form so that many people can relate to a style that appeals to them.

For some, it will be a reference book that helps explain the stages of grief. For others, it will be a tool that provides a sense of unity with others who have experienced the death of a loved animal. It may also be an inquiry into spiritual perspectives that are presented by animal communicators.

Crossing the Rubicon is designed to open the doors to healing on many levels. My hope is that this gathering of experiences will comfort you in your sorrow and lead to a healing celebration of the human-animal bond that exists beyond the death transition.

The following Relaxed Breathing and Tension Release activity, as well as the exercises at the end of each chapter, provide an inter-active workbook element that may bring up some powerful emotions. I strongly recommend that this book is used with the support of a qualified group, counselor or therapist who can help you through this process. The information, in itself, is an educational exploration and is not intended to be a replacement for professional counseling. If necessary, seek out an effective support system to accompany you on your journey.

Relaxed Breathing and Tension Release

It is useful to practice some form of relaxation that will help you open up emotionally to the workbook exercises at the end of each chapter. Deep breathing is very soothing on the entire body, and using a basic meditation technique works well.

Choose a warm, quiet place where you will not be distracted by external noises like the telephone, radio or T.V. Allow yourself enough time to complete each exercise without interruption. It is helpful to read the following guided meditation into a tape recorder so that you can be guided through the entire session while lying down or sitting in a relaxed position. If you feel uncomfortable with taping, consider asking a friend whose voice and manner seem soothing to you.

Before taping, take several deep breaths to relax, and just become aware of your voice, melodious and calm. Slowly read the words of *Part One: Relaxation*, allowing a few minutes of silence for each body area. Pause for longer silences during the quiet reflection of *Part Two: Visualization*.

This technique may take some practice. Be unstoppable in your quiet determination no matter how many times it takes. Everyone can succeed at this. Be patient with yourself and honor the process of discovery. It is essential that relaxation precede visualization, and therefore you should become comfortable with the relaxed, rhythmic breathing part of this exercise before moving into *Part Two*.

Part One: Relaxation

Close your eyes and gently breathe in through your nose to a count of six, hold for three counts, and breathe out through your mouth on another count of six. Hold perfectly still and focus on your breathing. Continue this until your breathing is as natural as possible without forcing a pattern.

Mentally visualize your body relaxing, one area at a time, as you feel your tension deflating.

Relax your toes. Relax the soles of your feet. Relax the tops of your feet. Relax your ankles. Feel the tension leaving as you think, "my feet are very comfortable and relaxed."

If a thought enters your mind, acknowledge it and let it pass. Follow your breath as you inhale comfort and exhale stress.

Now relax your calves. Relax your knees. Relax your thighs. Feel the tension leaving as you think, "my legs are very comfortable and relaxed."

Remain very still, and follow your breath as you inhale comfort and exhale stress.

Now relax your hips and pelvis. Relax your lower back and abdomen. Relax your mid-back and solar plexus. Relax your chest, your lungs, your heart, and all your other internal organs. Feel the tension leaving as you think, "my body is very comfortable and relaxed."

Let go of any distractions. Continue to concentrate, following your breath as you inhale comfort and exhale stress.

Now relax your fingers. Relax the palms of your hand. Relax your wrists. Relax your forearms. Relax your elbows. Relax your upper arms and shoulders. Feel the tension leaving as you think, "my arms are very comfortable and relaxed."

Visualize a sheer curtain and a light breeze. You are light as a feather as you continue to concentrate. Follow your breath as you inhale comfort and exhale stress.

Now relax your neck. Relax your chin and your lips. Relax your jaw, keeping a slight distance between your back teeth. Relax your ears, your nose, your cheeks. Relax your eyes and their sockets, your eyelids, your eyebrows. Relax your forehead. Relax your scalp. Relax your entire head, including your brain. Explore the orb of space from front to back, from top to bottom.

Feel the tension leaving as you think, "my neck and head are very comfortable and relaxed."

Remain perfectly still as you become your breath. Inhale comfort, exhale stress. Thank your body, and remind yourself that this is how it feels to be relaxed. It is now time to meet with your animal.

Part Two: Visualization

Become quiet and listen to your breathing. Let any external thoughts float through as you become peaceful in a comfortable rhythm of breathing.

Now visualize your loved animal in a happy and healthy state of being. Picture its healthy, glossy fur and see a white or gold light radiating around its body. Ask them where they are and slowly allow a sense of their surroundings to become clear.

Have a conversation of any length with your pet. Ask any questions you feel comfortable with and allow the answers to come to you. Allow quiet between the questions so that you can hear the answers. Tell your animal anything you have wanted to say.

When you feel the time with your loved one is coming to an end, be still for a moment, and thank your beloved animal for being with you.

Now, taking your time, gradually allow yourself to return to the room. When you feel ready, make some small circles with your toes and wiggle your fingers. After a few moments more, slowly turn over on your side or reach out and stretch like you do in the morning. After coming to an alert position, pause to reflect on all that has happened, and allow gratitude to fill you with a sense of peace.

Once you learn how to speak and listen in this way, you can have access to conversations with your loved animal at any time. Honor this conversation, because it is real. Do not allow yourself or others to make light of this important form of communication. It is sacred.

Crossing the Rubicon

Crossing the Rubicon

Chapter One:

The Grief Wave

Emotional Stages that Follow the Loss of a Pet

An Interview with Deborah Sullivan

Deborah Sullivan has been in practice as a psychotherapist for twenty years. Most of her work has been with adults, with a special interest in women's issues. Her primary treatment areas are depression, anxiety, trauma, chronic health and relationship issues.

It is important to understand the stages of emotional change that are likely to occur following the loss of a pet. So often we feel isolated in our grieving process and may be prone to feelings of guilt and depression. By understanding that there is a natural course of grieving that is likely to occur when a pet dies, we are better equipped to handle such changes.

The following stages associated with the grief wave have been adapted from the work of John Jordan, Ph.D.

The Grief Wave:
- Shock, numbness and quietude
- Yearning, searching, anger and protest
- Despair, disorganization and depression
- Reorganization and adjustment

The length of each stage varies depending on the individual. If your pet has been sick, you may have started the grief process prior to their death. It is important for you to know that this emotional response is normal, and should not be discounted with phrases such as "he is *only* a pet" or "it's *not* like she is a person." Rather, acknowledge the significance of the relationship with your animal. The most important part of any grieving process is to be able to talk about this significance.

It is essential to have other people in our lives who are supportive and understanding of what it means to love a pet. Very often it is helpful to have some kind of ceremony as a way to say good bye. One woman invited a number of friends and their dogs to her home when she buried her beloved dog. This ceremony helped her feel supported, which encouraged her healing process. Her friends commented that they were very moved by this get together and felt closer to each other as a result.

Another couple that I worked with felt that it was too painful to talk about the sudden death of their dog. During several counseling sessions, they touched on their sadness, but the wife avoided any further discussion because she felt guilty, maybe she could have done more. A few weeks later, they came to a session much relieved after finding a grief group for those who had lost pets. Both found much comfort in hearing others talk about their own sadness and guilt, thus recognizing that their emotional responses were not unusual. The ability of others to share feelings enabled each of them to express their feelings of sadness and loss.

Very often it is helpful for the person to bring in pictures of their pet and tell stories about them. This kind of reminiscing enables the individual to acknowledge what this relationship has meant to them. The stories tell a lot about the development and changes that the person and pet went through together over the years.

Some individuals will feel guilty about the grief they are feeling over the loss of a pet. They tend to discount feelings or attempt to move on without experiencing the feelings that are a part of this grieving. In therapy, it is important to have a safe place to talk about not only the grief, but also the idea that somehow we are being silly if we have intense feelings about our loss. Most people need to be reminded that the relationship they have had with their animal has usually been one of unconditional love on the part of the pet, and thus the intensity of that kind of love is a huge loss and should not be denied.

In general, grief takes as long as it takes. However, the waves of grief are less intense over time and the intervals between them lengthens. Grieving well means talking, sharing, receiving support, and often creating a ritual that allows you to thank that pet for all they have given you, as a way to say good bye.

When you add a new pet to your life, it is important to remember that this new animal will not take the place of your deceased pet. Rather, this is a new relationship that will enrich your life and bring new joy. Each animal has its own personality and you should not expect to recreate the same relationship you had before.

Brownie

By Terry LaMantia

It started much like the innumerable treks along segments of the Ice Age Trail in the beautiful Kettle Moraine area of southeastern Wisconsin. I said to Brownie, our chocolate lab mix, "Do you want..." That was the extent of the utterance and off Brownie ran to the garage door, whining and carrying on, before I could get out, "... to go for a ride?"

It was a warm September day. As soon as Brownie saw that the van was heading out of town to the narrow country roads north of us, she began to shake and pace. She started to talk to me and stick her big brown nose down my neck to urge me to hurry up and park the van by one of her favorite hiking trails.

After a fifteen minute drive, we parked by the trail head. Brownie bounded down the path along the edge of a cornfield and headed for the woods. The corn was browning and it rustled in the breeze as I briskly walked down the path in pursuit of Brownie who was almost out of sight by now. There was movement in the bushes on the other side of me and I saw birds flying to and fro in the thick cover, enjoying the last of the waning heat of summer. My eye caught a flicker of yellow as I hurried to catch up to my "Brown Dog," as we called her, who was now sniffing every sniff she could possibly possess – every animal scent, every plant.

We proceeded across the wooden bridge over the now dry swamp where we had found marsh marigolds the previous spring. We continued into the trees where the undergrowth was starting to prepare for the long winter season ahead.

Brownie was beginning to slow down. She had spent most of her energy in her enthusiasm to explore. She was becoming content to walk along and enjoy the smell of the still green canopy above us and the occasional decaying log next to the path.

We made a U-turn before we reached the first crossroad and returned the way we had come. We emerged from the tree line and into the cornfield. As we came into the open at our relaxed pace, I started to see what I had only glimpsed in the bushes on our way in. Brownie walked ahead of me and against her shiny brown coat were scores of yellow butterflies! As we walked along, there came more and more of them until there was a virtual drapery of yellow butterflies around us.

Today I can still feel the warmth of that wonderful day with Brownie. We lost her the following spring. When I think of her, I think of yellow butterflies and the brightness she brought into our lives.

Kate

Laura Borman

Kate was born on September 12, 1988 and died on September 14, 1995. Such are the meager statistics that ultimately sum up any life. My name is Laura. Kate, a Sable Rough Collie, and I belonged to one another. The statistics don't tell the story of how Kate gave the gift of her love and attention. Read on to learn about that.

As a pup, Kate was already developing the fiery, feisty personality that was to endear her to everyone who knew her. She had "snapping black eyes" to quote her breeder. This was actually quite an accurate assessment. However, Kate also had health problems from the start; she had early exposure to Lyme's disease, recurrent bladder infections and arthritis in her elbows already at six months. Given all these conditions, she must have been in a great deal of pain, even in spite of all the alternative health care. She never let her suffering show though, except in rare moments when the pain was probably unbearable. Her natural sprightliness and sunny disposition were her hallmarks.

Kate often seemed to be running and absolutely fearless; not even the intimidating vacuum cleaner scared her. Instead, she would valiantly do battle with it and subject it to numerous frontal attacks until it would give up and retire quietly to the corner where it belonged. The vacuum still bears battle scars from skirmishes with Kate.

She would smother those she cared about with love and affection. One friend of ours got the nickname "Collie Toy" because Kate would stake her claim on this lady's attention whenever she set foot in our house. Anytime was playtime for Kate, and she especially liked it if you would get on the floor and cover your head with your hands. You would then be treated to a volley of barking and tugs at your hair as she tried to make your head reappear. Her favorite activity was her walk, especially in a wooded park not far from our home. The walk had to be at the same time each day or Kate would get very insistent.

She was always beautiful and highly photogenic, but as she grew older she seemed to resent having her picture taken. Like a retired super model, her indignant and aloof attitude was obvious. Kate was highly intelligent and easily conveyed her message.

Whenever possible, Kate was given the opportunity to go where she liked without fetter. Usually this worked out all right, but as she got older and more confident, she began to go for unsupervised walks, always being careful to stay on the sidewalks. Supreme confidence was Kate's province throughout her life. She was well assured of her ability to accomplish whatever she wished, a quality I tried to nurture whenever possible.

With all of her independence, Kate was true to her Collie genetics and was always a babysitter. No one could be out of her sight for long. She was wherever you were; as long as she could see you and be sure you were safe, everything was fine. Kate and I were always together when I was home.

Her death took me very much by surprise. The continual bladder infections necessitated the use of an antibiotic that Kate had a toxic reaction to. One day she was running and playing; the next day she was desperately ill. I fought her disease with all the resources I could muster. It ultimately proved unconquerable and within one month, Kate was dead.

Kate's illness and death brought out some disturbing weaknesses in me. I was totally unprepared for her death since I had been fighting so hard to keep her alive. I fully believed that we would win the fight. So I felt responsible for her death, questioning the correctness of all the decisions I made. I was struck so hard that I strongly considered suicide just to be with my beloved Collie. The only thing that helped me was to stay with a friend who had also known and loved Kate.

At first, I couldn't even look at a photograph of her. That pain has slowly softened, but even now when I look at her I still feel a profound longing to have her with me again. I have another Collie now, and she partially fills the huge void that Kate left, but no dog will ever replace another. I found that many people have difficulty understanding the depth of feeling that surrounds a relationship like Kate and I had. They do not understand or cannot accept what Kate and I had all figured out and successfully lived. I will always be grateful for the loving and understanding that filled the time of our lives together.

Cissy and Megan

Barbara Ann Walsh

I have twice experienced the death of a pet. In both cases, I feel that I have been blessed because I have not had to make a decision about euthanasia and I have had a chance to say good-bye.

My first cat was given to me nineteen years ago by my father in an attempt to lessen my grief over my mother's sudden death from cardiomyopathy several months earlier. I felt a great deal of guilt over her death because I was a nurse, and I was sure there must have been something I could have done to save her. The antics of the new little kitten, and the love she showed me, brought a lot of happiness into my life.

When Cissy was two years old, she suddenly became ill. I took her to the animal emergency center where, ironically, she was diagnosed with cardiomyopathy. On her second day in the hospital, I went to see her, wanting her to know that I had not deserted her. I also knew that I would soon have to make a decision about euthanasia because the vet did not offer much hope for her recovery. She was breathing with great difficulty. I petted her gently and told her that I loved her and wanted what was best for her, but that I didn't know what that was. I stayed with her for a while and then left.

As soon as I got home the phone rang. It was the vet telling me that Cissy had died as soon as I left. I knew that she had been waiting to say good-bye. Cissy came into my life at a very difficult time and taught me that there are some things that we cannot control. Despite the best in veterinary care, Cissy could not be saved. It was foolish to believe that I could have saved my mother.

My second experience with death came when I had two cats, Megan and Caity. Megan was a sociable and loving companion who always knew instinctively when I needed her to provide comfort and love. She was ten when I was away on a business trip and had a friend watch them. When I called to check on them, he said that they were both doing fine. When I arrived home, however, Megan was not at the door to greet me. This was unusual. She had not held grudges when I had been away before. I found her in one of her favorite places and she seemed to be rather weak. She showed no interest in her food, which was very unlike her. As I watched her walk away from her food dish, she seemed to have trouble coordinating her legs. I feared that something was seriously wrong. With a sinking sensation, I took her to the emergency center.

She was diagnosed with kidney failure and placed in the intensive care unit. Over the next few days, she underwent numerous procedures. My emotions were on a roller coaster, depending on the current report from the vet. I went to see Megan every day and on the third day, I realized that I would have to make a decision soon. When I attempted to feed her, she spit out the food. I held her as I had Cissy, telling her that I wanted what was best, but that I wasn't sure what that was. I drove home crying and prayed that she wouldn't have to suffer.

The next morning I got a call that she had died during her morning exam. That evening while paying her hospital bill I met the vet who had been her primary caregiver. She showed me where Megan had slept and introduced me to people who had cared for her. They told me that despite the gravity of her illness, she was always at the cage door wanting attention and that she purred whenever they held her. They had tears in their eyes when they talked about her. In spite of my grief, I was touched by hearing how special she had become to those who cared for her in her last days.

That was seven years ago and Caity is now sixteen. She has chronic renal failure and I know that I will soon be faced with a similar situation with her. I have been asked why I continue to have pets, knowing their relatively short life span. Despite the deep pain that their deaths have brought, I would not give up a minute of the love and joy they shared with me in life.

Phantoms

Cheryl Sheehan

I'll find you drifting with the mist
Over the morning marsh,
Or racing storms across the sky —
Then following lightning to the earth.

I'll feel you in dim evening light
Settling in my heart —
Sweetly claiming space and time
As if we weren't apart.

Your dreams grow in my sleeping mind
Like spring on winter fields —
How gently, now, this mourning stirs
The place where you're revealed.

My Father's Dog

Julie Kaufman

My father is a psychologist. I have known him for almost thirty-six years. When I called and asked him to give me an interview for this book I was shocked by his response. "You mean you want me to talk about my dog?" I was temporarily speechless. After all of these years I had never known that my father ever had a dog. In fact, I had falsely assumed that he was less than fond of animals in general because he seemed detached and rarely mentioned them.

There were many Sunday afternoon visits when he had forbidden my brother from letting his dog out of the car on his property. In fact, he did not ever seem interested in animals at all except for the weekly riding lessons we shared at the local riding academy. We enjoyed riding together immensely, but I felt I was more attached to the horses as living beings. It was difficult for me to understand my father's apparent indifference because animals were central to my world. As a child I often wondered how we could be so different. I loved animals so much, and from early on I knew my life would be devoted to helping them.

After several moments of silent thought, I finally answered my dad's question. "No Dad, I wanted you to talk about the psychology of loss. But now that you mention it, I never heard you talk about having a dog.

And I want to hear about him or her." We agreed on a date for a visit. I was puzzled about the whole idea of talking to my father about this dog he had never once mentioned to me. He had actually commented, slightly critically, during our last visit that I seemed more interested in animals than in current events or the news. I had to agree that his observation was true.

It was fall when he came to visit. My father is a very intelligent and worldly man. I have rarely seen him out of control or highly emotional. But driving through the Wisconsin countryside, my illusions of him began to shake apart as I thought about him once loving a dog. He was accompanying me on my farm calls and as we passed the multicolored forests and fields, I asked him to tell me about the dog he once had.

He had lived in a very small apartment in the Bronx, New York, with his only brother and his parents. Also residing in the house for seven or eight years was his dog, Tippy. She was a little Fox Terrier mix who was very smart. My father never doles out accolades about intelligence lightly, and to hear him bestow such attributes to a dog was shocking and thrilling to me. He went on to tell how he would take Tippy down the three flights of stairs every day for her walks. He taught her tricks and she was his best friend. He explained how Tippy would sleep on the bed with him and look at him with eyes that were almost human. She was so efficient at communication that he never had to guess what she was saying. They were keenly connected in a way I have never heard my father speak of in regard to anyone or anything. It began to dawn on me that my father had never really gotten over the deep loss of Tippy's unconditional love and friendship fifty-four years past.

He continued to tell me about their relationship, teaching her tricks and loving her. I think I may have seen a small tear in his eye, and I have never seen my father cry. He then told me that one day she had to go see the vet, who found an infection that could not be treated. Tippy had to be put to sleep. It was so sudden. My father could not sleep for weeks. He thought about her day and night and expressed his deep misery following her death.

Thankfully, I now have some insight into this man whom I had assumed was indifferent. Perhaps he had never completely grieved her death. It was just too painful. To this day I think that my father has never loved anyone or anything as much as he loved his Tippy.

Chapter One

It is helpful to quiet the mind by practicing a basic meditation before doing the exercises. The suggested Relaxed Breathing and Tension Release techniques can be found in the front of the book in the Introduction.

Spend some time over the next few days looking for a natural object that reminds you in some way of your animal. It may be a rock, a piece of wood or another natural substance. Use this object as a point of focus whenever you want to remind yourself that your animal is always at your side in spirit. Carry it with you when you feel a need to be close to your animal. It will help you focus your thoughts and feelings.

Crossing the Rubicon

2

Chapter Two:

Options

Interview With Dr. Dawn Mogilevsky

by Julie Kaufman

Q: Can you give us a little background of your veterinary career?

A: I've been in practice nine years since graduating in 1990 from the University of Wisconsin, School of Veterinary Medicine. I have been exclusively in small animal practice for the last seven years, but my first two years out of school I was in a mixed animal practice. In the last few years I have developed an interest in holistic medicine. I specialize in acupuncture, and received my training through the International Veterinary Acupuncture Society. I find myself using more and more acupuncture, herbal and homeopathic medicines as alternatives to traditional treatments. This provides people with some additional options when conventional medicine produces undesirable side effects or where good treatment choices are few.

Q: As a holistic and conventional vet practitioner, tell us about some available options for the geriatric or seriously ill animal that may prolong or add quality to its life?

A: As our pets get older and their bodies start to fail, they may have problems with their musculoskeletal system because of arthritis or nervous system problems. Their ability to hold their urine and stool starts failing and many animals develop senility, anxiety problems or unexplained behavioral changes that are not very easy to live with. I also treat cancer patients, who may or may not benefit from available chemotherapy or radiation. As a holistic veterinary practitioner it is wonderful to be able to offer a client options in addition to conventional medicine.

With cancer patients, I can counteract some of the side effects of chemotherapy and radiation therapy using homeopathy, herbal remedies, and acupuncture. We can support the immune system, stimulate the bone marrow and appetite, help with weakness and reduce vomiting. I also see patients for which chemotherapy is not available, or cases where the client, for whatever reason, has decided not to pursue that route. In Chinese medicine, a solid mass or tumor is considered a stagnation of the chi or energy in the body. Using acupuncture and herbs we can stimulate and move the chi, strengthen the immune system, raise the individual's energy level and support their appetite.

I've had success using herbs and acupuncture to help pets with anxiety problems become calmer, enabling them to better function in their environment and to handle the stresses of daily life. Perhaps their anxiety was due to vision loss or associated with senility. I have patients who would have been euthanized because of their emotional discomfort or because they were not able to lead a normal role in the household anymore, and with holistic care we are able to extend their lives considerably.

Many of my patients have pain and loss of motor function from arthritis, trauma, or a ruptured spinal disc. I see significant improvement in patients that receive acupuncture, chiropractic care and various nutritional supplements to support their musculoskeletal system. Many times these are individuals who have exhausted conventional medical options. I have had patients who were paralyzed because of a spinal disc rupture and had back surgery, but still could not walk. Through acupuncture and chiropractic care, we were able to get those dogs back on their feet and walking again. There is nothing more rewarding than seeing a dog take its first steps. The relief from the physical and emotional stress and suffering is apparent from the joy in the faces of the people and their dogs.

Q: What are your views on the difficult subject of euthanasia?

A: The decision to euthanize a companion is based on a number of factors. Both the pet's health and the person's ability to care for them are important considerations. For example, when a large dog can no longer support its weight and get outside, it's just not possible to give it the proper care it needs. In some cases, even though we hate to admit it, finances are a significant factor. Sometimes the necessary treatment is just not financially feasible, and one has to be realistic about that. No one should feel guilty about financial constraints; we need to live within our means. By far and away the most important issue in my mind is the quality of life for the companion animal. I believe we're fortunate to have the option to end a pet's suffering when they're experiencing pain or have a serious illness with which we cannot help them.

It may be difficult to assess an individual's quality of life, and I get a lot of questions on how to know when an animal is suffering. It is important to consider their physical comfort and emotional state. Are they eating? Are they drinking? Are they responsive to their surroundings and interactive? Other factors involved when considering euthanasia are the types of treatment and diagnostic options available. For many illnesses there are good options, but other times the treatments are stressful or traumatic and can cause a lot of discomfort or unpleasant side effects without really offering much in the way of quality of life or prolongation of life.

In my mind, when an animal stops eating, can't move, stops having interest in their surroundings, it's really time to consider what's best for the individual. It may be time to let them go, and that's very difficult for most people to do. Some of my clients decide to euthanize their pet earlier than I personally would, and some of them hold on longer. I don't feel it's my place to make that decision. Each person needs to make the decision in their own time. What I try to do is present all of the options, make a true and fair assessment of an individual's condition, and offer them everything I can in terms of conventional medicine, holistic care, or a second opinion from a specialist at a referral center or university. Whatever decision the client makes, it's my responsibility to support them.

I feel when there is a lot of suffering or when we've run out of medical options that euthanasia is the best course to take. It's sometimes the kindest thing we can do, a final act of love to end a companion's suffering and let them go. Some people have feelings of guilt, which is a natural response. They wonder, "What if I had waited longer? Did I make the decision to let them go too soon? Would they have gotten any better?" I try to help people through that by first giving them all the options, and helping them decide whether those are good options or not. A person could spend all the money in the world and still not be doing what is best for their pet. I try to put their animal's condition and best interests first. If people approach it from that point of view it's a lot easier to deal with.

I have some clients that tell me that in retrospect they feel they waited too long to have their companion euthanized, but I don't recall ever having a client come back and say they made the decision too early. Obviously, we're dealing with family members that we love, and no one wants to let go before they have to, but it is important for us to let them go for their sake and not hold on for ours.

Many people have fears about what actually happens when an animal is euthanized, so I explain it ahead of time. I start out by asking if they want to be present when their animal is euthanized, or if they prefer to say goodbye first and leave them. Some people don't want to watch the process, but want to say goodbye or see them one final time after they've been euthanized. In that case I'll have them step out of the exam room while I perform the euthanasia. Then they can come back in and spend as much time as they need.

We give an intravenous injection of an anesthetic agent, and once the needle is in place there is no further discomfort for the pet. It feels the same as being put under anesthesia, just drifting off to sleep. It's really a very peaceful process. The dose of the drug is large enough to gradually suppress the heart and breathing, and then the animal passes on. Sometimes they will pass away very quickly, even before the injection is completed, and sometimes it takes a few minutes longer. It's unusual, but once in awhile we have to give a second injection if the circulation is too poor to carry the medication to the parts of the body it needs to go to complete the process.

I've found a number of people were distressed because they expected their pet to look like they went to sleep by closing their eyes. Their eyes stay open, so I forewarn people about that. I also tell them that sometimes the pet will vocalize just like a person will when they go under anesthesia. It doesn't necessarily mean that they're in pain or distress, but it's a normal involuntary event.

Once we finish the injection, I check the heart to make sure that it has stopped beating, and then I do whatever seems appropriate at the time. Sometimes that means staying in the room and consoling the owners, and other times it means leaving the room and giving them time to themselves. Some clients take their pets with them and have someplace that they want to bury them, and for others we provide a cremation service. There is the option of having a private cremation, and having the ashes returned for those people who want to keep the ashes in their home or have a ceremony to bury or distribute the ashes somewhere special. In certain situations I will make house calls for euthanasia, because some people find it easier to share their pet's last moments in their home. They do not have to experience any distress associated with coming to the clinic. These have been rewarding experiences. It is a serene and comfortable way for some people to let their friend go. For others, it would be an unpleasant memory to have their pet pass away at home.

Some people feel that no one should make the decision to euthanize, that nature should take its course, or depending on their religious beliefs, that God should make the decision when it's an individual's time to pass on. This is a struggle that people have to go through because, with humans and human medicine, it's so very different. Euthanasia is not an option.

There are very helpful support groups here in Madison through the University of Wisconsin Veterinary School for people that are grieving the loss of their pets. Anyone needing support should call their nearest university veterinary school and request information. There are also a lot of human care givers that help with this emotional support. No one should ever think it is silly if they're having a difficult time dealing with the loss of a pet. Many people think they shouldn't be so upset, that it was just an animal. But that's not true – it was a loved one, a family member, sometimes the closest companion in a person's life, and it is very natural to grieve them.

Q: Are the emotional experiences different for someone when their animal dies naturally at home without the aid of euthanasia?

A: It's a very different experience and gets back to a

person's basic belief about whether euthanasia is acceptable or whether nature should take its course. Many people comment that they wish they would just wake up one morning and find that their companion had passed away peacefully. To those people, a natural death would be a relief because it would remove the burden of making the decision to have euthanasia performed.

In other cases people can't bring themselves to let go of their pet. They delay the decision of euthanasia and their pet eventually dies at home. Those are the people that come back later and say they waited too long and wished they had not let their pet suffer. I think there can be regret and guilt that lasts for quite some time associated with prolonging the decision to have a pet euthanized.

Q: How long should someone wait to get a new pet after losing a loved one? What would you advise or caution against?

A: It's a very individual decision, and I don't really have any strong recommendations one way or the other. I have some clients who, after losing a pet, comment that they don't know if or when they'll ever get another pet. Losing their pet was too difficult. Then they show up in a week with another pet and say, "The house was just too empty. I just had to have another dog or cat or iguana or whatever." They are happier and it is nice if it eases their pain. It doesn't mean they are forgetting the previous animal, but building new memories can bring a lot of happiness into the home and help them not dwell on the absence of their first pet.

I have other clients who lose a pet that I don't see for several years. Then suddenly one day they show up and say, "It took a long time, but we were finally ready for another pet, and here we are."

Other people get a new pet when they feel their companion is getting older or ill. It helps them get ready for the loss, comforts them, gives them someone to share their love with. I've seen every imaginable situation and I think that each person does what's right for them.

Q: Do you have any personal spiritual or religious beliefs that you feel would help someone experiencing the death of an animal?

A: Spiritual or religious beliefs may help those experiencing the death of an animal, but each case is an individual situation. I don't know the religious beliefs of most of my clients, but I personally feel that there is spiritual life or existence for every living being that goes beyond our life here on Earth. I don't even begin to understand what that existence might be, but I do believe that our life goes on in some form. When an individual is suffering or dying, whether by a natural course of events or through euthanasia, I believe the spirit is released and is free to go onto the next life or form of existence, and that it is a beautiful experience. I believe that we will have contact with our loved ones that have passed on before us, and that it is a celebration to look forward to.

Q: Is there anything else you would like to add about celebrating the human-animal bond in life and death?

A: Celebration is a good word for the human-animal bond. For most of the people I deal with and for those who will be reading this book, I would like to emphasize that the animals in our lives are very important to us. They are members of our family, a part of our life that in some cases are our closest companions. That in itself is a celebration. When our pets are suffering for any reason, it's important to remember that we need to do what is best for them. The hardest thing we will ever do is to let go of these animals we love, to possibly make the decision to end our pet's life. It's because we love them so much that we must let them go. It's hard to do, and it should be hard, it should hurt to lose one that you love. It would be much sadder to lose a companion and a friend and not miss them or cry over it. We can celebrate death the same as we celebrate life, and look forward to the freeing of their spirit, the ending of their suffering. And I believe we can look forward to seeing them again in the future.

Several years ago I had a client who brought her cat to the clinic for grooming. On the way home in her car, the cat suddenly screamed and died. My client rushed back to the groomer, even though it was 10 o'clock at night. No one was at the clinic except the groomer, who immediately got a stethoscope, listened to the heart, and found that the cat was dead. They called me at home and asked me to come to the clinic to help. I found that the cat was indeed dead. This was a young woman who loved her cat immensely. The three of us went through many stages of the grieving process within a matter of an hour, from shock to understanding that the cat really was gone. Eventually we got to the point of talking about different events in their lives together, and we laughed and cried, and it just went on and on and around and around until we really had celebrated their lives together. It was a beautiful experience, very sad, but very beautiful, and I think it is important to go through that process whether it takes an hour or a number of years. This young woman was not done with her grieving by the time the night was over, but she was a long way into it. What helped was having someone to talk to who really cared and understood the depths of her feelings.

I would urge everyone to seek someone out you can talk openly and comfortably to about the depths of feelings about your animal companion. If that is a family member or friend, that's wonderful. But if not, seek out the help of a professional, whether they are a veterinarian or health care professional. They have a wealth of understanding and compassion.

Connor

Carmen Rasmussen

Connor was very unique in many ways. He may have been the largest Deerhound that ever lived. Along with tremendous size came a tremendous heart. Connor was a sweet, old, easygoing soul, and yet always a bit melancholy. I still keep a collection of his favorite toys in his honor. We called him the ambassador of giant dogs. He was huge, but not really scary. If you looked around back, that great big tail would be waving ever so slowly.

Connor had many trials and lived for four years with a tracheotomy that didn't seem to bother him at all. But being so large made it hard for him as he got older. He had been lame and in pain for awhile before we decided to do x-rays when he was six years old. Finding something in addition to his lameness or not, we had to face probably putting him down. The hardest part for me was not being able to feed him in the morning. When our vet called and told us it was cancer, it definitely was time. I brought him a piece of cheese which he was grateful for, sat with him in the run for awhile, and then he was peacefully put to rest.

We received so many letters, flowers and condolences. It was so nice to have that support. We still miss him, but are grateful that he spent his life with us. We bought Connor as a companion for our other

Deerhound, Dancer. They were great buddies and Connor was the only other dog that Dancer ever enjoyed. When Dancer died, I finally found an appropriate resting place for Connor's ashes, and that was on Dancer's grave.

The Dog Who Loved Too Much

Margaret Rowland

When I started editing this book it never occurred to me that I would include Tera's story. While talking with Julie one evening, I realized how close Tera is, despite the fact that she passed over some distant twenty years ago. Her story, our story, had been a source of guilt and despair, but I heard myself sharing it as my testimony to the enduring love and support that a pet offers.

She was the runt of the litter, a brown and black handful of curly Airedale fur. We were soul mates from the first time I held her. Tera means *earth* and I named her that because I felt grounded by her. Hours of quiet bonding passed as I weaned her from baby bottles and started her on puppy food. She was my shadow. She always found space near me, no matter how hectic things became. She was my constant companion and partner in mothering my young children. After our busy days, she would patiently and lovingly lay on the floor next to my pillow all night. Our bond strengthened as time passed. When safety or security were in question, she would nobly and calmly be at my side with her low assuring growl. We had grown accustomed to each other.

One day we were outside and I wanted to leave for the grocery store. I asked my daughter to take Tera inside. She walked over to her, but before she could grab her collar – it was over! Her friend, not knowing, had stepped in and grabbed Tera's collar to help my daughter. Tera bit her because she was a stranger. The child's arm was bleeding. Her mother came. She had stitches. My daughter and I took over a get well gift. All the while, I was frozen with fear. Would they report her? They didn't, but my head swam with fear filled thoughts. Would she do it again? How could I make sure she didn't? Extended family members echoed my worst nightmare. "Put her down," they said. "One bite is never the last." These conflicting forces fought a war inside me for weeks. Then one day Tera and I went to the vet. I came home alone. I abandoned her. She never would have abandoned me. To the contrary, she loved me too much.

For over twenty years, I have carried and buried the pain while questioning the necessity of my decision, possessing no way of knowing *what if?* And now, after telling Julie, my pain has lessened. Somehow, I always knew what I was about to hear. Drawing on her metaphysical intuition, Julie confirmed that Tera had indeed been special. So special that she sensed Tera's energy by my side as she had been for some twenty years now, my spiritual companion. She is happy and understands what I did. Finally, as I write this, I write with a renewed and happier heart that our bond was never broken. Death stole her body but not her soul.

Frewin
My Free and Noble Friend

Maia Michalsen

My baby died on July 15, 1997. He was a year-and-a-half old. All my dreams and my worst nightmares came true during that time. The night he came into this world, my friend Stacey and I were there to help. He was just as I had hoped, a dark bay colt. I named him Frewin, which means "free and noble friend." My life seemed to take a leap forward. Things were starting to finally go my way.

I never really felt like I could get enough with him. I have had horses all my life, but he was so different. When I wasn't at the barn, all I could think about was sitting in the field or just hanging out with him. He loved to play chase with our dog, running and running – God how he loved to run. He won First Place at his first horse show. I will never forget that day. He was being a brat. In the stall, he wanted to play. I hate to say it, but I did get annoyed. In our class, there were seven or eight yearling colts, but all eyes were on my baby. He knew this and he performed like a total gentleman. I told him how proud I was and that, in my eyes, he was the greatest. I didn't need a ribbon to know that he was pure gold. The judge wrote on his card, "He is going to be a good one." That was my first and last time showing him.

Frewin had a retained testicle and gelding was a concern. It shouldn't have been attempted. Things went badly when the vet started to geld him and I ordered the vet to leave my land and never come back. Freewin was shaking and covered in sweat and foam. It took three hours for him to let me near. I decided that he would never have to go through that again.

A month later, I contacted a well known equine vet. He examined Frewin and said a castration would be nothing at all. He couldn't do it at my place. I needed to go to a clinic for my own sense of safety. I remember how good Frewin was that day. We waited together in the trailer. I admired and comforted him. Since I wasn't allowed to stay I put Frewin in the stall and said, "See ya later baby. " I didn't want to leave him. The vet assured me that he would be fine.

On my car phone I was told, "We lost him..." The rest of the day is a blur. I remember throwing up on the side of the highway. I remember begging my dead baby to get up. I stayed in bed for days. I lost the one thing that completed me. He was my friend, my partner and my son.

It has been a couple of months now and the pain is still raw. At night, I am haunted by the dream that he is lost while I keep searching for him. Some days are better than others. On the good ones, I can remember and love him with a smile instead of a tear. The road has been hard and I still have a long way to go, but I am not alone in the journey. I have good people around me and Frewin is around too. Some days when I go to the barn, I glance at the pasture and I feel him there. I hear the faint thunder of his little hooves and I can almost see a glimpse of him racing through the pine trees.

I thank him for coming into my life and I send my love and smiles to him. I know now that he is gone from this world, but he will always be with me.

Frewin

Sue Daubner (Maia's mother)

There is no card to ease this pain
No cutesy word, no slick refrain
No flower's fragrance can assuage
The numbing loss, the hurting ache.

There is no answer to the "Why?"
A special love like this should die
Sometimes a glimmer of light will shine
A reply to our anguish, a balm to our mind.

No spoken word or look can tell
How to escape this private hell
This Calvary's trail you're treading once more
Gets no easier for having been trod before.

He'll be with you always, within your seeing
Within your heart, your mind, your being
The love you gave, he gave back to you
Know now it will flower and return anew.

He won't let you go, not ever, but trust
This pain will diminish, for as with all
Things unbearable, it must.
Try now to live each day one at a time
Knowing that life does not always justly rhyme.

The rhythms it keeps are not ones to know
But keep the memories to soften the blow.

Time in the Tiger's Eye

Julie Kaufman

It was 2:45 A.M. precisely when the howling pierced the silence like a long thin sliver splitting the barrier between light and dark. How could she have known the meaning of the words promised in a whisper hours before?

Lucy was a four-year-old feline in full glory. Her gold and white tones were divided in patterns only Leonardo DaVinci or God would have been talented enough to design. Her grace evenly matched her stunning physical appearance.

I loved to visit the comfortable "kitty palace" that was home to Patty and her husband, Karmjit, and their five cats. Not only did Karmjit love the animals, but he also had a passion for flowers and the necessary green thumb. Each spring, the front yard was a living sea of tulips, and Karmjit seemed to capture some of Lucy's beauty and color in his garden.

When I called, Patty told me the news. Despite her healthy appearance, Lucy's diagnosis was a seal of death, a type of lymph cancer which quickly takes the life of the animal. Patty and Karmjit were given the option of chemotherapy or euthanasia. They knew that Lucy's time was very limited and felt comfortable letting Lucy be put to sleep when the time came. We talked about Lucy's gorgeous green eyes and long flowing coat which was marbled so beautifully and how it was just a matter of time before Lucy became a light body, releasing her beautiful physical form.

A few days later, Patty called me. Lucy was deteriorating rapidly and beginning to show behavior indicating that death was near. Patty found Lucy laying in the fireplace alone and barely breathing, and she was cold and unresponsive. I suggested that she call the vet. We talked about how Lucy's death would impact the four other cats. They knew that Lucy's time to cross over had come. They all loved her, but were avoiding her to give her room to die.

Patty phoned me later that afternoon and again I urged her to call the vet to see if anything could be done at this point to help reduce Lucy's suffering. They took her in and she was given fluids, which seemed to increase her energy. Unfortunately, she lost the energy later that evening. The couple made the final decision that it was time to let her go.

They phoned the vet one last time and arranged to put Lucy to sleep at 2:45 the following afternoon. That night the house was finally quiet. Lucy was in their bedroom, but the others stayed away. The digital clock read 10:30 as Patty rolled over and whispered a promise, "Just hang on, Lucy. Please just hold on till 2:45 and we'll help you go."

Lucy heard and understood. She hung on. At precisely 2:45 A.M., she cried a piercing howl. Patty never thought to tell her she meant P.M.

Her passing was a calm relief. Lucy's struggle was as courageous and noble as her spirit. Patty and Karmjit buried her under the tulip bed, so in the end, Lucy returned in multicolored perfection. There she shone flowing into the visual spectrum and radiance that she brought to all of life in a new form.

Chapter Two

It is helpful to quiet the mind by practicing a basic meditation before doing the exercises. The suggested Relaxed Breathing and Tension Release techniques can be found in the front of the book in the Introduction.

Relax and breathe. Think of a decision or circumstance with your pet that you have not fully processed. Are you ready to let a little more of it go? If not, move on to something you are ready to release. It may seem small, but don't let that stop you. How can you gift yourself by moving forward through painful thoughts of a past event? Share your insights and the action you take to release those thoughts with someone you love.

Crossing the Rubicon

3

Chapter Three:

Letting Go

Interview with Dr. Heather Evans

by Julie Kaufman

Q: What is your background?

A: I received my doctorate in veterinary medicine from the University of Tennessee College of Veterinary Medicine in 1994 after completing a bachelors degree in Animal Science. I discovered my interest in animal acupuncture while working in a holistic veterinary practice in Minneapolis, Minnesota. I completed certification requirements for veterinary acupuncture from the International Veterinary Acupuncture Society (IVAS) and have been studying and performing acupuncture in Milwaukee, Wisconsin since 1995. Through training from the American Veterinary Chiropractic Association (AVCA), I have also become certified in animal chiropractic. Recently, I returned to Minneapolis, Minnesota, and am currently offering acupuncture, chiropractic, herbal therapy, nutritional counseling and Bach flower essences for our canine and feline companions.

Q: What are your spiritual beliefs?

A: My spiritual beliefs have evolved somewhat from my upbringing with the Christian church. I feel a strong connection to Buddhism and Native American traditions. I sense that we are all connected, not only with fellow human beings, but with the animals, plants, earth, and sky. I believe in my heart that all beings have souls and every spirit is special in some way. Through death, friends (both human and animal) that have left us in body come to visit us through dreams, visions, and within other beings.

Q: How do you explain euthanasia to your clients?

A: When explaining euthanasia, I tell people that I feel it is a gift... providing relief from suffering for our animal friends. The euthanasia solution is injected into the vein and travels through the bloodstream to the heart. The process is very quick and essentially painless. I tell people that the animal may take one last sigh, there may be muscle twitching of the body or limbs, and the eyelids may or may not close. In some situations, the animal may go through an excitatory phase during the injection. The animals may whimper or cry a bit and move their limbs. This reaction is due to the chemicals in the solution. Although I have never experienced this first hand, I will make people aware of it so that if it does happen, the client will be prepared. I think that as long as people are aware of what may happen during euthanasia, everything goes rather smoothly. It is when something happens that surprises people that this procedure can be traumatic for both the patient and the client.

Q: What emotions can a client expect to experience?

A: The emotions expressed are as varied as the people who experience them. I find that all people feel sorrow and loss, although people express it in different ways. There are also feelings of guilt and regret. Some clients go through a period of reflection, questioning if they did the right thing or if they could have done more for their animal companion. I have rarely seen anger expressed over the death of a euthanized animal. I feel that if those closest to the animal are in agreement over the decision to euthanize, and if they feel that they have done everything possible for their companion, angry feelings are minimal. With time and emotional support, we begin to realize that the decision to euthanize an animal companion was made out of love and respect for the life of the animal.

Q: How does this differ from a natural death?

A: Euthanasia differs from a natural death in two ways. The first difference is a physical one. When a natural death is occurring due to chronic disease, the dying process can be slow and lingering. People witnessing euthanasia for the first time are often surprised by the quickness and peacefulness of it. The second difference is an emotional one for the person. I find that people struggle more with euthanasia because they are making the conscious decision to end their animal companion's life.

Q: How does the client know that it is the appropriate time to euthanize?

A: Because I practice alternative medicine, many of my patients come to me with chronic disease. I rarely see animals under the age of four and most of my patients are well into their middle aged years. I love working with the "geriatric crowd" because they are so wise and appreciative of anything I can provide them. They know that I am working with their human "mom" or "dad" to provide a better quality of life for them. So, with this type of practice, I talk about euthanasia a lot.

I always tell my clients simply this... when the bad days outnumber the good days, it's time to think about euthanasia. Of course, when I say this, I am talking about chronic disease... having a terminal illness that cannot be cured. I will oftentimes have people write on their calendar or use a wellness journal to document good days and bad days.

Most people know when it is time. When their animal companion stops doing his or her favorite things (for dogs, it's usually eating and tail wagging, and for cat's, it's social interaction), it's time to think about euthanasia.

The MOST important event in this process is letting go. The client must verbalize to their animal companion that it is okay for them to leave. This heart to heart talk gives the animal the freedom to die in peace and helps the person say goodbye. I have seen animal patients remain with us simply because their person will not let them go. Some of them seem to feel a duty to stay, particularly canines. I must also stress that it is important to tell the animal that if he or she wants to stay awhile, that we will do everything we can to make them comfortable.

Q: How long should someone wait before getting another pet?

A: This decision is a very individual one. Some people find another animal companion immediately and others wait. I mention to people that they may want to look for an animal companion that is the opposite sex, a different breed, or another color. Then again, I have a client that is currently living with her second German Shepherd, both named Rocky. She enjoys reminiscing about the first Rocky while giving treats and attention to her second Rocky. My advice is that when you think you are ready, open yourself up to it, be receptive, and the right one will come along.

Q: *Anything else to add when celebrating the human/animal bond?*

A: We are truly blessed when these wonderful animal spirits choose to spend their lives with us.

The Odd Couple

Bobbi Mallace

She was a little shorter, rounder and plumper than the rest of her Lowchen litter mates so she was appropriately named Miss Piggy. Teddy, her brother, was a bit taller and thinner. Miss Piggy was slower to react to things. Teddy was very bright and quick. These two were our *odd couple* who went everywhere together, side-by side.

Through the years Miss Piggy and Teddy spent much time together – playing, wrestling, arguing and eating (which was Miss Piggy's favorite sport). They socialized with the other dogs in the house as well as with the family, but they always seemed to do it together.

As they approached "middle-age" I noticed that Miss Piggy would lag behind Teddy at times. She no longer ran at his side, but stayed close behind him while Teddy periodically checked to see if she was following. We wondered why Miss Piggy would do this. We received the news from our local vet that Miss Piggy was losing her ability to distinguish objects, but would be able to see strong contrasts of light and dark. "Of course," I thought, "Teddy is black so she is able to follow him." For the next few years, Miss Piggy would follow Teddy everywhere and they seemed as though they were glued *head to rump*. In spite of Miss Piggy's impairment they were quite the happy couple.

One day, Teddy just stopped eating and appeared listless, but the vet could not find anything specifically wrong. The problem continued in spite of trying different medications and diets. After extensive testing we were told he had cirrhosis of the liver and had only a short time to live. Every time we had to take Teddy to the hospital, Miss Piggy would howl and cry for several hours before she would settle down. We decided to bring Teddy home and let him spend the time he had left with Miss Piggy.

Six weeks passed and Teddy seemed very comfortable and comforted by Miss Piggy. They didn't run anymore, but cuddled up together. Then one day Teddy stopped eating and began digging at the floor. He dug all day only stopping when we called his name, but then he would continue on his mission. We tried to comfort him, but he would have none of it. We would learn later that in the wild, a dog will dig a nest in which to die. Miss Piggy became very quiet and left Teddy alone. She knew what was going to happen.

Around two o'clock in the morning I got up to check on Teddy. He lay very quietly, as though he had worn out his body digging. I detected a faint heartbeat and called the vet who told us to bring him to the hospital, that he would meet us there. As I picked up Teddy I realized he was no longer in pain or discomfort – he was gone. Miss Piggy was very quiet and wanted to be left alone. When we took Teddy to the hospital this time, she didn't cry or howl. This time she understood.

Miss Piggy grieved for many months. She began to try to find her way around without Teddy. Slowly she learned to follow one of the humans who lived in the house. She never adopted another dog to follow, although there were several from which to choose. She now appears to be relatively content and we help her as much as we can, both physically and emotionally. We spend time cuddling and talking to her, but we know she will be the happiest when she finally goes to be with her beloved Teddy.

Roscoe

Richard J. Binder

Roscoe was born in a little gray cottage nestled under towering weeping willow trees. The cottage was located next to our three bedroom ranch house in Glendale, Wisconsin, a suburb of Milwaukee. My sisters, Kathy and Liz, picked him out from the litter and brought him home where he was immediately welcomed by our family of eight – Mom, Dad, Kathy, Liz, Mary, Bob, Tom, and me. Our one-eyed cat Nicky, however, never fully appreciated him. He had run away for two weeks when he was just a kitten, but returned one day after a terrible fight, battered and missing one eye. He was king of the house and although Roscoe was seven times his size, he remained King for the twelve years he presided over our family.

Roscoe was a Collie/German Shepherd mix, more beautiful than Lassie. We thought he was the nicest and most beautiful dog in the whole world. Liz helped train him to heel with a towel that he bit, instead of using a leash. He could do all the tricks: sit, lie down, roll over, stay. My favorite was to have him sit-stay while I put a piece of cheese on his nose. When I said OK! he would flip the cheese into the air and catch it without fail. Roscoe's favorite toy was a tennis ball, and we always had a full stock of used balls for him. I would use a racket to hit them as far as I could in the back yard, up over the telephone wires and into the neighbor's yard. Roscoe would fetch the balls and never seem to tire. He also had a rubber ring that I would use to swing him around in the air while he held on with his mouth. He absolutely loved it!

Although he lived in a house with eight people, and Nicky, our cat, Roscoe was painfully shy. When my parents had big parties, Roscoe would stick his head under a table draped with a cloth that hung to the floor in our living room. The rest of his body protruded, but Roscoe felt secure in his little fort.

My parents would take Roscoe for walks around our neighborhood that had no fences and very large lawns. Roscoe would run in and out from behind the houses, racing through all the yards as my parents walked and talked. None of the neighbors ever complained and Roscoe was in heaven.

Most evenings the whole family would sit down for dinner and Roscoe was allowed to sit next to the table and wait for scraps. My father, who was a gentle yet quietly demanding man, liked to pretend to ignore Roscoe. But he knew better, and always sat next to my father, who would then sneak him food when he thought we weren't looking.

During the winter, Roscoe would sleep on the floor with his back against the front door because it was cool. We liked it because he seemed to be protecting the house. My older brother and sisters, Bob, Kathy and Liz, eventually grew up and moved out of the house. When Bob moved back home from college to take a job in Milwaukee, he stayed with us and Roscoe got to sleep with him on the hideaway bed in our family room. On the weekends his wife Therese would come home from school in Madison to stay, and then Roscoe had to sleep on the floor. This was the only time I ever saw him get mad and sulk. Poor Therese, she was the nicest person and we all loved her, and so did Roscoe until those weekends.

Roscoe aged gracefully. We moved to a big two-story house with a stairway and landing. Roscoe would sit on the landing and look out the window over the driveway. He was always there in the window to greet you when you came home. My mother didn't seem to mind his nose prints and smudges on the window and sill. This was Roscoe's spot.

He always seemed healthy except for the ear mites he got one year. He hated the medication, when we'd have to hold his head and fill his ears with goop. He never got used to it. Luckily the mites cleared up. Then one day we noticed a tumor on his stomach. We had it removed and they told us it was benign. But Roscoe's stitches wouldn't heal, and he was very lethargic. Then we heard he had lymph cancer. It progressed very fast.

The night he died I slept with him on the floor. My parents woke me in the middle of the night and told me to go up to bed. They moved him to our front hallway where he passed away. When I woke up, Roscoe was gone. My father had to bring him to the vet during the night. We were all very sad.

For months afterward, I would still hear Roscoe come

running whenever I opened the refrigerator or cookie jar. My mother missed him terribly during the day when everyone else was away. Although it is twenty years later, I still relive fond memories of Roscoe. He was a very important part of our family and we all miss him.

I Lay You Down To Rest

Mickey Hopper
I wrote this after having our thirty-four-year old gelding
put to sleep last month

Spring begins to raise her pale green leafed head
The sun shines a little warmer, and a little longer
And earth begins to yawn and stretch
Awakening from a wintry nap

Grand old horse, you stand still
With a far away look in your eye
Long winter white coat has begun to fall away
And your rich Palomino gold shimmers

Do you recall days of glory
Ribbons won, prancing to a parade band's beat
Jumps conquered, and trails explored

But wicked time has pulled your legs out from under
you
You lean on the wall to rest
Afraid to lay down
That you might not rise again

No carrots, no hay, just special feeds
No more rides, back swayed
Your legs cannot bear
Every breath a battle
Every step taken a risk

The last gift that I can give
Is rest
To lay you down
Never more to struggle to rise
On shaky legs
Never more to moan in fear
That you will be trapped

Rest now
Lay down your head
And breathe one last sigh

I will plant a willow above you
And when it blooms
I will remember a day
When you stood in tall grass
Rose gold among the green

And the sun shone a little warmer
And a little longer
And spring had just begun to raise her pale
Green leafed head

Daydreamer
—For Muffie

Amy Crane Johnson

Old dog,
what doggie dreams
do you dream as you lay
in the sun and a smile
strikes then drifts
across your face?

Do you dream
of fields of summer grasses
that beg to be trampled
and a sky so bright
you feel alive in your bones
and run without restraint
until your master commands
your return?

Maybe that smile
is in memory of the boy
who fiercely loved you until
an inkling of girls brushed
his consciousness, leaving
only his boy scent embedded
in your mind and in his quilt
where you huddle at every chance.

Do you dream
of past lives where Emperors
cherished you and sleep
came on silken pillows near King's heads,
of Chinese palaces, where a bark
from your black lips
brought jeweled swords
to attention at your ruler's side?

When you shiver in your sleep
is it the frozen land of Lhasa
that only through instinct
you can remember? Or is it the chill
of the silver tub where the boy
used to wash and scent you, taking
out the animal smell
and with it the loss
of part of yourself?

Old dog,
when you smile
that smile
what doggie dreams
are you dreaming?

Picture of Cat

Elisabeth Johnson, age 10

Cat with hollow tail

sits silently wondering

what it would be like

Thank Your Lucky Stars

Julie Kaufman

Kathy was one of my favorite clients. She was kind, considerate and gentle. How could I say no to her? She was asking me to see her mother's twelve-year-old Collie. Lucky was overweight and had severe hip arthritis, which made walking impossible for the past six months. Kathy's mom, Dorothy, was struggling with both his care and the idea of losing him.

All three of them were in the examining room down the hall while I was looking at Lucky's x-rays. He had one of the worst sets of hips that I'd ever seen. One of the vets in my office walked by and remarked that maybe I needed to talk with the client about the options. I collected the paperwork and slowly made my way toward the exam room, stopping at the door to gather my thoughts and emotions. When my voice broke the silence, I somehow managed to sound less emotional than I felt. Dorothy, who was cradling a handful of used tissue, immediately starting sobbing. My eyes then dropped to Lucky, who was quietly watching from a blanket on the floor. He looked at Dorothy with deep concern and attentiveness. His tri-color coat was still healthy and glowing, despite the overweight status of his body spreading over the blanket.

Lucky was alert and in seemingly good health, except for the fact that he obviously couldn't use his rear end at all. I knelt down to greet him while I ran my hands over his body. I began to take notice of muscle loss, hot and cold spots, reflexes and overall health. There was a lot of muscle loss over the pelvis and rear legs, which were not strong enough to support the weight of his body. He also seemed to have pain in both hips where the muscle was waning.

Dorothy started to talk as I explored Lucky's body. She told me that she wasn't ready to lose Lucky, but that her husband wanted to put him down. Between sobs, she told me that he didn't understand how much Lucky meant to her. I showed them Lucky's x-rays and regretfully informed them that I didn't think there was much I could do, given the severity of his hip condition. I pointed to the illuminated film of his hips, demonstrating how hard it was to tell where the ball ended and the socket began. Most of the hip joint had fused together. I described the severe pain that accompanies advanced arthritis, and finished by saying that they should consider what was best for Lucky in terms of quality of life. The subtle allusion to euthanasia was lost in the emotional torrent.

We were in the room for almost an hour. Lucky looked around anxiously at the three of us as if he understood every word. I looked into his eyes and saw a spirit willing to go on, if only he could find a way. Every now and then, one of the vets would peer into the glass window. They seemed to be waiting for a signal to perform the inevitable procedure of putting Lucky to sleep.

I finally knelt next to Lucky and agreed to try two treatments, but only on the condition that they consider the options if there was no improvement. Dorothy gladly welcomed the reprieve. I began the chiropractic adjustment on Lucky and was able to restore motion in several places, praying as I moved through the procedure. Lucky stood the treatment well, and started to look like he was enjoying it. He licked his paw and relaxed tremendously.

Then something miraculous happened. Lucky looked around, took a huge breath and hoisted himself up on all four legs!! We all gasped and stared in astonishment as Lucky looked attentively at the door leading out of the clinic and barked loudly. Dorothy cried with joy this time.

I was probably the most surprised! I had convinced myself that it was hopeless. But Lucky taught me a lesson of the highest order that afternoon, one that has stayed with me each moment of every day. None of us can assume to know what the plan is. We need to do our very best and never give up. The rest is up to nature and we need to not stand in Her way.

Lucky lived a quality life for another seven months. He had his ups and downs, but mostly he was up and around. This gave Dorothy time to prepare to say good-bye. I miss Lucky terribly, but I thank my Lucky stars to have been a part of such a miracle.

EXERCISE

Chapter Three

It is helpful to quiet the mind by practicing a basic meditation before doing the exercises. The suggested Relaxed Breathing and Tension Release techniques can be found in the front of the book in the Introduction.

Sit quietly and relax. When you are ready, recall a memory of your loved animal in which you experienced unconditional love, a memory that makes you feel lucky to have shared this with another being. Recall the specific colors, smells, sights and sensations, and the exact feelings you had. Spend several moments in the reverie of this love, being grateful and saying thank you to your animal. Then take this memory and share it with another.

Crossing the Rubicon

4

Chapter Four:

Into the Light

Death From a Spiritual Perspective

Interview with Adrienne Martin

By Julie Kaufman

The following is taken from an interview with Adrienne Martin that was done especially for this book. She is a clairvoyant, which literally means "clear seeing." She is also clairaudient which means "clear hearing" and clairsensient which means "clear sensing." These abilities are best described as an intuitive sense of knowing things before they happen. They have always been available to her, but after being teased by her family, she stopped paying attention after age seven or eight.

She started paying attention again a few years ago when her son, who was seventeen at the time, committed suicide. She started using all of her abilities after his death and made a commitment to be open and listen. At that point, information just started "pouring in." She now uses her gifts to benefit humanity and animals. She was first asked what an animal experiences at the time of death.

A: I will just say that pets are really no different than human beings and it is just a leaving-the-body experience. The spirit leaves the body and the soul's energy is completely available to us, the same way that there is no death. From what I see and the reality that I deal with everyday, we don't die, and the same is true of our pets. Their spirit leaves the body and they go through a tunnel and up into light and are then completely available to us from this other dimension. They come through to me on my screen between my ears right in the center of my head when I close my eyes. It's an energy that is available to the person or animal that I'm reading. There may be some animals that take a longer transition, so they don't immediately go through the kind of experience that I just described. They may just be in limbo, they are just resting awhile. They may have had a shocking kind of death and they need a little time to get adjusted.

Q: When they leave their bodies are they assisted spiritually? Do humans and animals have guides, spirits or some entities that would help them along? What would those entities be like?

A: I don't know if I can say for sure because I have not seen or experienced an animal guide, but I have experienced the animals in the same space as humans, in the same vibration and on the same level of energy.

Q: So pets go where humans go?

A: I don't even know if I know where humans go. They both come through on the same rate of vibration. And I can say assuredly that they are being assisted, because it is difficult to reappear. It takes some energy and there has to be a big want to, a desire to. So, love is love, from a pet to a person, from a person to a person. It's all in the same dimension on the other side. It's all love. Love is how we bring a loved pet through – their love for you and your love for them and they are very tuned into the vibration.

Q: Do you see pets reincarnating? If so, do they reincarnate as pets or can they be other pets? Can they be humans? Do the souls cross over that way?

A: Let's take a dog as an example. The dog will leave this lifetime as a dog and come back as a different dog. I don't see that they change species to humans, at least I have not had experience with that. They might come in as a different breed of dog. They keep evolving and there are levels of evolution for each species. There is learning that takes place. There is a sense of their knowing, and you know if it's a wise dog. Sometimes I'm in the presence of a very wise dog and I am very clear that the dog has been here many other times and has learned how to do this love thing.

Q: So the bottom line is really lessons about love with our animals or humans?

A: Exactly, yes. Animal-human, it is very related.

Q: What can owners do to help the animal who has just passed to find peace, and to also find peace for their own sake?

A: Allow them to be gone. Send them energy, light, love and help them experience moving more quickly through the transition. It is difficult because we are grieving over our loss and perhaps it really isn't a loss, but just a change. I mean it's not a loss in that they are still completely available to us and we can talk to them if we so chose.

Q Why is it so difficult to accept that life may go on in a different form?

A: I have my opinion. I think that preventing our believing that there really is life beyond death has its roots in religion. Historically, some religions wanted to control humans, so the idea and the concept of the possibility of life in a different forms were stopped way back.

Q: Can you talk more about that? I don't want to get off on this too much, but what are some of the reasons that some religions attempted to cut people off from God? Essentially, why would a religious organization want to control humans?

A: Probably for the same reasons that we want control in our own lives. It is always a control thing, and a lower level of vibration that doesn't allow people to transcend to a higher place. It is the same as we can do while living on the earth plane. We can transcend up through different levels, gradients of interaction in our own lives. But we will keep ourselves at a lower level of vibration through these control issues. If we are trying to control an issue or event, then it doesn't have nearly as much capacity or possibility of evolution or movement upwards in terms of gradients.

Q: Does it matter whether we cremate them or what is done with the body? After death, is there a certain period we should wait before we do anything? How does all that work?

A: Good question. Once the spirit has left the body,

it doesn't make much difference. Do what you wish for your own healing and needs.

Q: How long does it take for the spirit to leave the physical body?

A: Seconds, but there is another concept to consider. There is energy still left in the body. The spirit has gone, but there is still energy on the body. So, the familiarity that an animal or person has with their body would have them perhaps come back to that body, not into that body, but around the body. If you thought you were in tune enough and that you might encounter that person or pet, look around the body or their familiar surroundings. It's all got energy and they'll be vibrating at that level of vibration. They may appear to you or somehow communicate. Somehow you might get a communication from them. They may just shake the shades or do something in an area where they have been used to being.

Q: So they could leave a physical sign?

A: Yes, it is possible, depending on their level of vibration and capacity to do so. If they weren't really sick, they might still have a lot of energy, even though their spirit left their body. It depends on that energy. I am very clear from what I see on the spiritual plane that people and animals go to the same place or are vibrating at the same level (rate of vibration) when they show or present themselves. I can sometimes hear them. I hear dogs barking and cats meowing. I can also see them. They show themselves to me, and bring themselves through on all those different levels of vibrations.

Q: *So again, the biggest favor we can do for our pets when they pass away is not to keep them from evolving or moving forward. How does that work with our grief work and wanting them back in our lives?*

A: Well, as humans we feel uncomfortable or sometimes avoid being around somebody who is grieving heavily. It is a difficult energy to be around. Try to just BE WITH the grief or sorrow and celebrate the contribution they made to your life. It is the same with a pet or person that has crossed over. It is difficult to come and be with you when you are in that lower vibration of grief. There is nothing wrong with it, it's just more difficult and they don't want you to grieve. They are in this great place and are so happy there. They are not bound by their body.

Q: *Is it possible that a human or animal could die and not know they were dead and perhaps get stuck?*

A: Very possible, yes. I don't want to say the transition is difficult, but sometimes it can be so quick that the reality shift doesn't come along with it and it takes awhile to adjust. I just use the word adjust because it is an adjustment. They are trying to communicate in the old dimension while they do not know how to communicate from the new dimension. It will feel to them like they never changed dimensions.

Q: *Will the other helpers on the spiritual level be able to successfully bring them to the higher vibration eventually if they are stuck?*

A: OK, now that's a different thing than if they are

over there and they're not sure where they are and haven't adjusted. If they have actually made it over, then they've made it over. There are beings who do get stuck and are confused and will stay more earth-bound. They will stay closer to the earth and not have the possibility of this full transition to make it over to the other side. They stay stuck in earthbound and that is where you get the term "earthbound entities." They need our love and prayers to help them fully cross over.

Q: Like poltergeists or that sort of thing? Is there any way to know if that does occur, how you could help your human or animal become heaven bound?

A: Yes, the access for them is the light. You can help them by sending them light and asking them to move into the light. It's harder for them, so a lower vibra-tion, a poltergeist kind of vibration, will mostly be doing things that aren't good and that don't make you feel good. If you don't feel good about it, the odds are very high that it is an entity that has not been able to cross over fully.

Q: The best thing is to offer light and ask them to move into that light?

A: Yes, surround them with light. Ask them to go to the light. Be very clear with them. Make it very clear that this is in their highest good.

Q: Is there anything else relating to animal death and dying that you want to share? If someone want-ed to find an animal communicator, or someone who has gifts such as your own, to help them understand their animal's death, how would they be able to find someone?

A: A good, reputable spiritual psychic will know that we can "tune in" with animal vibrations. I think that word of mouth is probably the best form of reference. It's just like anything else, if they've been recommended on some level, it is a bit easier. It may be a little risky, but you might find someone good through advertisements. I would add that psychics or mediums who are spiritualists, who have been trained as readers of psychic energy in the spiritualist tradition, would be very good people to contact.

Bruiser, My Best Friend

Sue Heilberger

"How fortunate I am to have a best friend like you, Bruiser..." I often told my Golden Retriever this as we sat at Lake Michigan during our daily walks. We truly were the 'Best of Friends'!

Several years ago, I noticed increased panting at rest and during activity. I became worried, as this was not his normal health state. I took Bruiser to the veterinarian who had cared for him over the past eight years. Bruiser was diagnosed with allergies and given respiratory medications. This treatment did not change the intensity of his panting.

My level of concern and anxiety was heightening and I sought out the services of a holistic veterinarian. She examined him and said, "I think that I can help Bruiser. He seems to be experiencing symptoms related to hip displasia." Those seven words gave me such great hope for my best friend. Now it was my turn to watch over and care for him, as he had done so many years for me and my family. I truly felt blessed to have found this wellness center and the practitioners who performed their interventions on Bruiser.

The following two-and-a-half years were filled with many ups and downs, but Bruiser always responded to the treatments. During this time I felt that God had given me the chance to take time out of my schedule to devote to Bruiser. How else could I ever return even a small portion of all the kindness he showed us and the many lessons we learned about unconditional love.

This time period was also filled with much discomfort. I thought a lot about Bruiser dying and experienced a lot of anticipatory grief. Most often the thought of losing Bruiser would cross my mind and I would cry or feel very anxious. If I wasn't with him, I made decisions to cut short my errands and return home. I started to worry about the possibility of Bruiser dying alone and I felt so worried and helpless as I did not know when he would die. I could see that after the two-and-a-half great years of an enhanced level of living, Bruiser was not responding to treatment as he had earlier on. I felt so helpless at this stage of his life. After much thought during our final walks together, I knew that I just could not prolong his suffering. When the time came, I prayed for the opportunity to be with him and comfort him.

On July 8, 1998, my best friend went to Dog Heaven. He was eleven years old and had suffered a mild stroke. My husband, daughter and I spent over two hours with the vet who gave Bruiser his two extra years of wellness. We decided to euthanize him, a decision that did not come easily or painlessly. We sang "You Are My Sunshine," his favorite song, as he died.

I have never felt such pain and loss in my life. I have been blessed by a dog angel who taught me about forgiveness, commitment and unconditional love.

"I miss you Bruiser (UBU). May you enjoy and heal in heaven."

Memories of Mitzi

Kathy Agenten

I love you so! We met when you were the smallest Miniature Schnauzer pup at the breeder. You caught my eye and captured my heart. We became soul mates from the first, sharing a perfect relationship. You worshipped me, while I adored you. You were my dream come true, my own sassy, loving puppy who was always ready to greet me when I came home.

There were so many little things we enjoyed. You taught me to take time to sit with you in the warm summer sun and to rock you to sleep in the glow of a peaceful winter night's fire. When I went to visit at the nursing home, you came along and brought your own brand of joy. The residents' faces would always brighten up when you'd wag your tail or give them a kiss.

You taught me so much, especially when you had health problems. We learned sign language when you lost your hearing. You taught me to see only your inner beauty and look past the tumor on your hip. I learned to look beyond the physical to the spiritual. Thank you.

As you grew older and more sickly we knew our time was short. You spoke to my heart in so many ways. Your increasingly frequent signs of illness often put a lump in my stomach and a coldness in my heart. Your last three months I watched as you slowed down. As Christmas approached, we knew it would be your last. Our time together became even more special. I remember you sitting beneath the shade tree and watching me ride horses. I focused on you to put it deeper into my memory because I knew we would not have many more of these days together.

Finally one Monday morning, God told me it was time. Our dear friend and vet said he would come out to the house since you were always so scared to go to see him. Despite the fact that I wanted your suffering to end quickly, we would have to wait until that afternoon. Thank God for that last beautiful day together. We sat in the sunlit grass while I comforted you and told you how much I loved you. We went for a ride in the golf cart. When the vet finally arrived, he put you to sleep in my arms. It seemed so natural, just how you had fallen asleep so many times before. God answered my prayers for you to go painlessly and fast. After you died, I still held you and stroked your tummy the way you loved so much. Your spirit had not left yet. But then your life was over, and a wonderful part of mine ended also. Finally, I knew the time had come, and I buried you beneath your favorite shade tree by the barn.

The following days were every bit as heart wrenching as I thought they would be. Thankfully I had friends and family who understood, and no one said you were "just a pet." Our relationship was only ten years long, too short, and yet longer than many marriages. Outside, I saw you everyday as I passed your grave. You sleep there now, just like you used to at my feet for hours on end. Many times, I still looked for you in the house. You weren't there, but at times I *felt* your presence. You were there, I know it. Two days after you died your spirit left the house for the final time. I felt you say good bye. I put some of your hair, your picture and a story about you in a safe deposit box. I wanted to have these things safe and there to read and touch whenever I needed to.

That was three months ago. When I think or talk about you I still cry. When will the hurt stop? I know time will help to heal my pain. I hope to soon forget the hurt. The memories, especially from your final day, give me comfort. My prayer was for God to take control of the last day. He did. It was wonderful, beautiful and comforting. I can pass your grave daily now and not cry. I think of you often.

God giving you to me was a great blessing. I have learned not to grieve for your passing, but to rejoice in your having been here. I know you are in heaven because God loves you and all other animals. When an animal dies and is grieved, indeed she did her job on earth well. Thank God for all the memories we made together.

You were my pet, my companion, my friend, my love. Good bye my friend. We WILL meet again. I love you so.

Aftermath to Mitzi story:

I've had Pixie, a Miniature Schnauzer, for nearly two years now. The exceptional bond I had with Mitzi that I feared I would never again have, I do have. Time, an open heart, an understanding God, and a loving Pixie have again blessed me with that heart-filling bond. I am truly grateful for these blessings.

The Super Dynamic One

Sindy Smith

The Visits

(Told by Julie Kaufman)

This is a story about a beautiful Irish Setter named Rosebud. I will tell of her passing over and subsequent visits to the people she loved, Sindy and her friend Tony. In the last few years of her life, I spent many hours with Rosebud and her human Sindy. When Rose asked Sindy to help her cross over, Sindy asked me to be there with them.

Dr. Lepar gave Rose the injection that would help her leave her body. It was a quiet act of love and mercy. As Rose took her last breaths and passed quickly, Sindy and I held her body and cried. Almost immediately, I sensed that Rose's spirit was at peace and full of joy, running in tall green grass. There were many, many, many spirits there helping Rose. Her body seemed light and untouched by the physical pain and weakness she had suffered in her final days.

The First Visit

As I drove home after Rose had joined the spiritual realm, I saw a brilliant sunset filled with reds and oranges. This was such an unusually red sunset with neon-like qualities. Somehow I sensed and saw Rosebud in all of her glory flying through that evening sky. I sensed that she was relieved and filled with peace and joy. Rose thanked me for being there with Sindy at the time of her passing, and I was able to say a fine good bye to this beautiful spirit.

The Second Visit

Sindy told Rose to tell Tony that she was full of joy and at peace. She stayed with Sindy for a few minutes until the sun went down and then she was off. Tony later told her about his experience with Rose, which happened only minutes after Rose left Sindy. Tony felt a vast burst of joy-filled energy running around the yard, and knew it was Rose. She entered the house with Tony and ran around filling the house with peace. He went to lie on the bed and Rose joined him, telling about how happy she was, and that she wanted him to understand she had to leave her physical form when she did. Rose shared a sense of healing with Tony. She stayed about fifteen minutes, and then left.

The Third Visit

Sindy had to make a number of calls about Rose during the days that followed her passing. She remembers getting through them, but finally bursting into tears after the last conversation. As she wiped her tears, she was filled with and surrounded by Rose's peace. Sindy acknowledged her presence, picked up one of her toys, held it close to her heart and laid it on the couch. Sindy was enveloped in a warm sense of healing for several minutes.

The Fourth Visit

Sindy was playing with the sugar gliders (small marsupial animals) while she thought about and missed Rose. She wanted Rose to know that she didn't sense her presence as much as she used to and that she missed her deeply. Rose immediately surprised Sindy with her presence and told her to stop playing with the gliders. But Sindy asked Rose to bless the gliders coming into their lives and give up her old resentments. Sindy explained that she needed their companionship as well as Rose's visits. Rose then seemed to understand and accept them. Sindy remembers feeling a deep emptiness. Despite her loneliness, Sindy told Rose not to return in another physical form before she was ready. Now Sindy waits and looks forward to Rose's return.

The Fifth Visit

Suzanne, Sindy's sister, said it was an average evening. As she looked up, she saw a healthy black Irish Setter shadow bouncing around in the next room. Rose said hi, that she was OK, and full of joy and peace. Then she said good-bye and departed.

Rose traveled near and far to many others she loved, letting them know she was fine and bidding them farewell.

The Sixth and Final Visit

Tony felt Rose's energy force enter the house one day and sit on the couch with him. The energy was so strong that he embraced it and told her how much he loved and missed her. She gave him some kisses in return. She said that she liked being with Sindy and Tony and wanted to come back again as a red dog. She said that she was almost ready to come back. She said she was going to visit Sindy, but asked Tony to call first and share her message. All weekend, Sindy fought the urge to call Tony. On Monday she was looking at Rose's picture, telling her how deeply missed she her. Rose told her that she would be back, and it wouldn't be much longer. When Tony and Sindy later talked, they shared their similar experiences and were filled with joy. The similarity confirmed that Rose would be with them physically again soon.

The Return

(Told by Sindy Smith)

The joy of Rose's physical return cannot be measured. It makes for a much deeper and richer companionship right from the start.

The first time I went looking for Rose in another physical form, I went to see some pups. I held a few, but didn't feel anything. I sat back and looked at all the pups, searching for a sign that one was Rose. One pup's face had a certain glow and made me think of Rose, so I picked her up, connected, and told her I would be back when she was ready to come home.

Four out of the six females were spoken for. I prayed that divine order would bring us back together. As time grew near, I had some doubts and fears in my ability to connect and choose the right pup. I prayed that it would happen and kept repeating that divine order will make it happen. I sent messages asking Rose, my *Dynamic One* to give me some strong signals when I came to pick her up. On November 23, 1997, I prayed for guidance and went to pick up my pup. I asked Suzanne, my sister, to go with me as she might sense or see something that I might miss. And I wanted the extra support.

When the two pups were brought out to choose from, I became very nervous. I had to relax so I could receive messages and connect. My first clue, or message, was when one pup went over to Suzanne and kissed her glasses, which was a notorious Rose trait. The second clue was when the breeder asked me what I was going to name the pup. When I replied, "Sindy's Diana Rose," the pup turned and looked at me from across the room with full attention and said, "I'm here." One pup was dynamic and the other was indifferent. Knowing that I made the right choice (and Suzanne agreed), we left for home with my new companion. Suzanne drove to give me time to bond with and console the pup on the beginning of her new life's journey.

As I carried Diana into the house, she glanced around the room and said "Good, I'm home." Diana was calm and peaceful the first night away from all she knew. The second night she wanted to play when it was time to sleep. I put her in the kitchen and told her if she was going to play during sleep time she would have to sleep alone. As I walked away she vocalized and sent the message "You said you were going to treat me better this time." I smiled, laughed, and took her back to bed. Each new day brought more messages confirming that she, Rose, was back.

Having a return makes communicating and training easier and speeds up the process. Sometimes it's like having an old dog in a puppy body. Sometimes I would hear Diana thinking about the things she had to learn again. At times she was upset with herself about the things she should have known. Having a returning spirit is a wonderful gift! Indirectly, I did buy Rose a new body. I thought I could not do that when she was alive the last time.

Oh what joy! I also found an Irish Setter for my father which turned out to be the spirit of my first setter, Tammy. When he had her put to sleep, I had invited her to come and join with Diana as another animal companion, if they both agreed. She did, and now they share the same coat and make Diana *The Super Dynamic One.*

Thirteen Grams

Amy Crane Johnson

You told me once that if you died
first, you'd be my guardian angel,
making sure I'd pursue life
and not follow you into the unknown.
You said you'd sing me to sleep
with off-key tunes
so I'd be sure to know it was you.
That would be a heavy burden
I laughed, hoping
I wouldn't have to find out.

And now I'm told the body loses
thirteen grams of weight
at the moment of death
and science believes this thirteen
grams is the exact weight of the soul.
They even have scales
to measure this type of thing
and a small needle
registers the loss
as the spirit lifts away
from the body
leaving only an earthly
bulk laying there on a cool, white sheet.

I know this could be true
for at times I feel your presence
riding my shoulder, sitting near my broken
center, a heaviness I can't explain.
It's then I think I hear you
as I'm giving in to sleep,
under a concrete blanket of death,
thirteen grams more or less
a weight I can almost bear.

For the Love of doG

Julie Kaufman

Based on Chelsea's life

I am a Bull Mastiff named "Chelsea." My human's name is Melissa. I want to send an important message from the spirit world to anyone who has ever known the love of a doG on earth.

Before crossing over to the spirit world, I shared nine loving, wonderful years with Melissa. We had great times together and I cherish each one. I really miss her cooking and our cuddling up on the bed after dragging the clean laundry around the house. Sometimes Melissa and I didn't see things the same way, but our love endured and grew as a result.

One of my favorite memories is when she took me to her friend's ranch in Kansas. It was really flat for miles and the cows were just standing around, surely waiting for me to start some chasing games. Since I was free to run, I chased them, and they started to run and kick up their heels. We were having such a great time, so I couldn't understand why Melissa and her friend were so upset with me. The cows seemed bored before I got there.

I also remember playing with my cat friend, Pootie. We used to take turns knocking things off the shelves in the kitchen to see which ones would break. My mom didn't seem to understand this game either.

One time someone brought a big, delicious cake over when we had a party for our neighbor, Julie, who was graduating from chiropractic college. They set the cake down right in front of me! How could I resist? It was great until I got caught with icing on my face.

Time flew as we shared our love, and my body began to slow down and ache. Near the time of my passing, I couldn't get up and move around anymore, which made my mom really sad. My memory is a little foggy, but I do remember asking her to help me go because I was ready. She understood, and took me to the vet who kindly helped me out of my misery.

When I left my ailing body to rest, shedding the weight of my physical form, I wanted her to know where to find me. I came to her in dreams and thoughts to tell her about the angels who lifted me gently, light as the breeze. I wanted her to know I did not feel any pain, and that I was happy and alive in my new, lighter form. I saw her crying over my old dog suit and I tried to lick away her tears, but she could only hear me softly and thought she was just wishing I was there. I really was, and I loved her as much as ever.

Now I can see the whole of my life, its purpose and design. I can see each kind thing she did for me in such a loving way, and all that I gave to her in love. I know there were things we wish we had done differently, but those are so easily forgotten here. We were earth angels for one another, sharing joy and love in a crazy world. But the world is where we can learn all about choosing love, where we realize how hard it is to live in hate and anger. Now I have graduated into the spiritual world, where I can see the big picture. It is very simple, really. It's all about love.

I want Melissa and every other human companion out there to think on these questions so you will know what's important: Did I make your life a little easier? Did I make you laugh at my goofy tricks and wild play? Did I make you happier to wake up each day by greeting you with a lick and a happy wag? Did I love you no matter what mood you were in? Was I successful in my earth mission? Soon I will rest before choosing another purposeful mission in another physical form, another dog suit. Please do not forget me or the love we shared. Try to remember and recreate it in your world. It will mean so much more if you keep the love we created alive and share it with those in need.

By the way, God tells us doGs that you can't really tell who needs love just by looking at them. Humans are kind of funny that way, so like us doGs, that you just have to offer love to everybody. That goes double for humans who act like they really don't need it, so be especially loving to mean or crabby people. I will be wagging my tail for you and smiling at the gifts you are sharing with humans who just haven't experienced doG yet.

It is more in a doG's nature to forgive and forget, and God sent us to you to teach you this lesson. After all, God is doG spelled backwards, and you thought we were just mangy mutts! Let the love we shared rip. It is time to heal all of the wounded souls who are in pain. They may not have been as fortunate as you and I who have experienced the love of doG.

Thank you for hearing me, and please remember me always and share the love I gave. I will not forget you. I am watching and guarding you from my place among the angels. The love we shared in life is embedded in our soul's fabric. Don't forget the love of doG.

P.S. There are even cats here, and we all get along just fine.

EXERCISE

Chapter Four

It is helpful to quiet the mind by practicing a basic meditation before doing the exercises. The suggested Relaxed Breathing and Tension Release techniques can be found in the front of the book in the Introduction.

Think of something you are ready to forgive yourself for. It may be something seemingly small. Imagine a large ball of pink light surrounding you and include the action, words, or feeling troubling you. Now watch the pink ball of light gently lifting up and carrying off whatever you are ready to let go of. Allow it to float up ten feet, twenty feet, and follow it up through the clouds and beyond. Follow it up until it breaks free in the highest part of the starry sky and becomes transformed into light burning within the core of a star. Surround yourself with a clean and fresh white and golden light. Say out loud several times, "I forgive and release those things which are no longer for my highest good. I choose instead to focus on the goodness and purity of my being." Breathe and enjoy a sense of being cleansed. Repeat this exercise often when you feel burdened or heavy.

Crossing the Rubicon

5

Chapter Five:

In a Different Voice

Interview With Asia Voight

By Julie Kaufman

The following is an interview with Asia Voight, who is an animal communicator.

Q: What drew you to this field?

A: When I was young, I was really close to the animals, understood them, communicated with them just as naturally as breathing. And it wasn't until I got to be about nine or ten that I realized nobody else talked to the animals. And I just somehow knew that I wouldn't be believed or understood or that it was really unusual. So, I let go of that. And then I had a car accident eleven years ago. I had a partial hearing loss, which forced me to start to hear in a different way, and I started concentrating, and all of a sudden I was hearing the animals talk to me again.

Q: What does that voice sound like? How do the animals come through to you?

A: They have different voices. Some animals are really excited and say things like, "Hi, this is who I am and this is who I like," and are very animated, with different personalities – just like people have.

Q: So is it mostly auditory for you, you hear their voice for the most part, or do they also send pictures?

A: It's a combination of voice, picture, feeling in my body, and even taste sometimes.

Q: What kind of things would you taste?

A: Actually that's probably the one that I have the least experience with. I was working with a cat, and I said I would like to experience taste. He said okay, and all of a sudden the cat went after a fly, caught the fly, and it was buzzing around in its mouth. I could feel the fly in my mouth, too.

Q: Oh, how weird.

A: Yes, it was kind of disgusting. It was like, I got it. And sometimes when I'm working with horses and they say they like certain treats, like "I like root beer barrels," I can taste it perfectly in my mouth.

Q: How can you tell the difference between being able to know that your communication from an animal is real, versus an imagined communication?

A: Interestingly enough, using your imagination is part of the spark to getting connected. When we were children, we were encouraged to use our imagination – it was part of the right of being a child, the freedom, the magic, the mystery, the unknown. It's like a little spark, an opening. And so using your imagination is the first step to connecting with animals. It frees you to not be wrong. When people feel they're going to be wrong, they tighten, close up, become frightened. They don't want to be wrong. But just use your imagination, and since it's "not real," you can't be wrong. And it's fun just to be more free. I open my mind and my heart.

Your third eye opens, and your heart opens, which is part of what you can use to communicate with the animals, to get on a different level, like a vibration. But using your imagination is the opening. And then the other part of that is, when I'm really centered and relaxed and down in my body along with the opening or spark of imagination and allowing that information to come, it's the most correct, the strongest, clearest connection I get, versus when I'm grasping or guessing. That's when I've been wrong instead of being patient and relaxed and open, allowing the information, the communication from the animal to come. And it's a very strong knowing, a very clear hearing or a very sharp picture.

Q: What percentage of the time would you say good communicators are correct? I'm sure even the best people sometimes pick up misinformation. Is it possible for an animal to lie to you?

A: I feel that eighty-five to ninety percent are pretty accurate. Sometimes I've been with animal communicators who are probably 100 percent correct. But the part where you might not be completely correct is, for me, when I haven't asked the next question.

Another situation that comes to mind is these people who were testing my abilities to see if I was a true communicator. But it was kind of funny, because they were talking to their horse, telling their horse what to say. Don't you think that's a little ironic?

Q: You mean because if they don't believe in it yet, then why would they tell their horse something, thinking you're going to hear it?

A: Right. They told the horse to tell me that his favorite color was pink and purple. So, this is the test. I talked to the horse for about an hour. Finally, they asked me to ask the horse what his favorite color was. And when I heard gold, it was really deep and very strong and steady. It was gold. And I was actually just going to stop there. But since the horse did not offer pink and purple, I just happened at the last moment to ask, "Oh, is there any other color that you like?" And it said, "Oh, yeah, pink and purple." And his voice was really high and kind of wavy, and it wasn't until later on that I realized that I should have asked why his voice was different. Then maybe he would have told me, "Oh, they told me to tell you this even though this is really not my favorite color. " So see? Sometimes it's not that the animal's lying, it's that you didn't ask the questions in the right sequence to get to all the information. And sometimes they just don't offer it.

I've had other experiences, like when the animals play with me a little bit. And sometimes I catch it and other times I don't until maybe halfway through the reading, I'll ask, "Why are you doing this? Is this really true or are you exaggerating a little bit? Is this part of your personality?" And then they admit they were playing.

Q: *So animals can exaggerate or sometimes even manipulate a little bit?*

A: Yes, but not generally.

Q: *They're pretty clear?*

A: Yes. I think how they're seeing it is that they don't withhold. I mean, some animals even have a full swearing vocabulary, but I don't know if they learn it from humans.

Q: *It could be. Well, let's talk about the subject of death and dying a little bit in terms of questions that people may have about euthanasia, whether that's okay with animals or not, and of the process the animal goes through. How do you know when it's time to help your animal with euthanasia? Are there some clear signs and symptoms that you can let people know about?*

A: What I normally find are obvious physical signs at the point when I'm called. The animal's either moving slowly or not breathing well. It's obvious ill health or very advanced age. And I will then ask the animal if they're ready to pass on. It seems to be a combination between the animal and their human, if that's going to happen. People are much more tied and upset then the animal is. Death is a much bigger deal for people because of the fear or hesitation or just not wanting to go through the grief, just wanting to have their animal to stay with them all the time.

I did a reading for a woman the other day whose dog has a very serious heart condition. She's known this for a year, and has been healing with the dog and doing beautifully until about a month ago. And this dog has a hard time breathing. So when I asked this dog if he was ready to go, he said, yes, but he knew that his companion was not. And so I worked with her, and she said, "I feel that I'm really ready to let him go now. He's suffering. It's very hard for him to see me, every breath, I'm tense."

So we worked back and forth in conversation. And finally the dog said, "O.K. you know, I just want to die, kill me." It was very strong. And she was shocked, "What, just kill you?" It was hard to hear it in those terms. Sometimes we like to use words that soften it, like "put them to sleep," "euthanasia," or "passing over." Sometimes people need to soften the words and that's okay. But the dog said, "Kill me. If I was out in the wild, I would have already moved myself to a place where I would have died."

Q: Animals sometimes knowingly walk into their death?

A: Yes. About six months ago, a woman's dog was very unhappy in their relationship and their situation, and the dog asked if it could change. And she said, "No, absolutely not." She was very rigid and unwilling, and no matter what type of situation that I suggested, she was unwilling to change at all. While she was saying this, you could see the dog become more and more depressed and sad. He just flopped down on the ground where he had been walking around, hopeful that something would change. By the end he was completely depressed and went off and just laid down in a corner. About a month later, he ran in front of a car and was killed.

Q: Oh, no. Almost like a suicide.

A: Yes. And this was a dog that had been through extensive obedience training; he was one of the top obedience trained dogs in the area.

Q: So he knew about cars.

A: He knew about cars and about the risks and he ran out in the road right in front of a speeding car.

Q: Wow. I've actually heard some other stories along those lines.

A: And he had said to me, "Well, if she's not going to change, I'll find another way." But I didn't ask what that meant because we were just ending the reading and she said that she needed to go. But then when I heard that he had run in front of a car, I realized what he had meant. It was really shocking.

Q: Yes, I can imagine it's very shocking that way. So it's important to listen to our animals, too, when they're ready to go?

A: Right, right. But I think that was an unusual case because it seems that the dogs and cats and horses are so willing to work in a loving, patient way with their human companions. But this had been going on in his life for about five years.

Q: Oh, I see. It was a long term thing?

A: Right.

Q: It is also important for the owner to be ready to let the animal go, even when it can be very difficult to work through the grief. What are some of the things that people can do to prepare for an animal's death? Anything that you can do in addition to just going through it and getting some support or counseling?

A: I have my own beloved dog who is reaching the age of twelve. I love her so much. And what comes into my mind that is really reassuring for me as an animal lover is a call I got about six months ago.

This woman's dog had been running in a field and suddenly had an attack where it was not able to move or get up. And followed by that was erratic breathing. So I talked to her over the phone and was able to get a very strong and clear connection with her dog. But what surprised me was that I saw the dog laying with her on the couch, and about three feet away were three beings that I would describe as angels, just standing there. I asked them, "Will you move forward and do some healing work for the dog and this woman?" They said, "No, we're just here to wait for the dog to decide what he wants to do. He's right at the brink of death, and if he decides to pass over, we're here, ready to take him to the light, to the other side, to a very beautiful, wonderful place. But we cannot intrude at this point; it is up to those two to decide."

So I asked the dog, "Do you know that these angels are waiting here for you?" And he said yes. I asked him what he was going to do, and he said, "Well, don't you think that my companion would be very upset if I left? Because she just lost her horse of twenty-five years a year ago. I think she will, don't you?" And I agreed that yes, she will. She will be very devastated to have two of her beloved companions die within the same year. And he said, "I don't want to do that to her, and I'm going to stay."

Q: How interesting. So free will really plays a lot

into whether the time is going to be now or later.

A: Yes. He said he would do everything he could to live through this time, and thought he could make it until morning. And so I sent my blessing and love to him, and said that I would check on him in the morning. And when I checked in, he was doing very well. And then I called, and sure enough she said, "We sat up through the whole night with him just praying and doing energy healing work, and he pulled through amazingly well this morning."

Q: So there was really a window where he could have died, and he chose not to?

A: Right. It was so reassuring for me to know that there was that space between here and there. He knew that there are spirits or angelic beings or other family members waiting to help and to be right there. So not even a moment has to go by when there's not a loved one with them.

Q: Oh, that's wonderfully reassuring. What is "over there?" Are you able to see what "over there" is? What happens to an animal during the death process and after they die?

A: I can talk about it in two ways – one from my own experience of the car accident eleven years ago, having a near death experience and remembering when I died, that everything wasn't "up there" or far away. It was actually sideways. And it was only a breath away or an inch away from here. And it was surprising to me that it was that close. It's very close.

When I crossed over, I was instantly greeted by angels

and a loving pink glowing light that encompassed my whole body. Every cell of me knew unconditional love and peace that I have never experienced here on earth. And I felt more alive on the other side than I do here. I don't have any more fear about death or dying.

I try to help the animals with that. And some of them have really clear memories that they have had many lifetimes, and some of them aren't sure. They ask me, "What is it like, what's going to happen?" So I tell them about my experience, how loving and peaceful and joyful it was, and how, if their body is suffering and uncomfortable now that this pain will not follow them, that they will leave that behind and will be in their spiritual body, which then can run and jump and move easily. I just remind them of that.

I recently had an interesting reading with a woman and a number of her animals who were still living. She said "I have a dog that died a year ago. Would you contact him?" I asked her to give me a picture and tell me his name, but not to tell me anything else about him. I wanted to challenge my skills and make sure that I wasn't being led by anything she told me about him. So, I did my grounding and centering exercises and called for the dog. I saw this big, white dog coming, but he could barely move. He had hip dysplasia, but I couldn't tell if it was the right or the left side. And then I clearly felt it in both hips. I told her this information and she said, "Yes, exactly, it was in both hips. He could barely move by the end of it." I described his personality and she got tears in her eyes and said yes, that it was him.

I went on and was very surprised when he led me to a large cave. On the outside of it was a spiral ledge, and there were hundreds of mostly dogs and cats sitting there. He said, "I have been sitting here waiting, and she says she hasn't decided if she will ever get another dog again after me." I told her this and she wondered if that had anything to do with it. So I asked him and he said, "Yes, my heart was broken when I died. I loved you so much and did not have a long enough time with you, so I've been waiting and hoping that I would be able to go back to you again. But because you were undecided about getting another animal in the near future, I didn't know what to do. So I've been in this space of just waiting and feeling this grief and sorrow."

I told her this, and she said "Oh, my God, I want to tell you that I just bought a farm with some land and now I will have space for you and, yes, I want you back." And in that moment he got up and said, Okay, follow me, I'm leaving here. I don't need to be in this place anymore." And out of this cave we went into a beautiful garden. Right in front of me, he transformed out of his old body into the body of a little bouncy, white, fluffy puppy saying, "I'm going to experience this joy and love in this garden now, but I can come to you in about ten or eleven months." She said that sounded wonderful. And off he went.

Q: Oh. So there is actually a place of "in between" where spirits can stay for a period?

A: Yes. She was really surprised that he had gone there, because she actually does hospice care with people and had used some of the techniques on her companion when he was dying, such as saying, "You're free to go, you've been loved here, and there are other things waiting for you on the other side." She was really surprised that he didn't directly go there. But because his heart was broken, he decided not to, that he'd just wait and figure out what he was going to do. He wasn't suffering, but he definitely was not all the way into the light where he ended up.

Q: Can you talk about how animals feel about euthanasia generally?

A: Yes, A woman came to me and said, "I have a horse that I had to put to sleep three years ago, and it has been a burden on me ever since. I'm wondering if you can help me." So we set up a time and she brought a picture. But when I called for the horse, it was behind me hiding, kind of peeking out. Normally I see them in my mind's eye coming forward through light. So when I told her this she just started laughing, saying, "That is exactly my horse. That is him, because when we used to look out into the pasture, he wouldn't be there. We would call and he would come peeking out from behind the tree or the barn. He was always playing this hide-and-seek game." So that was his way of saying, "Yes, it's me."

I relayed to him how upset she'd been over the last three years and asked him if he was angry at her. He answered, "Oh, my, not at all. I wish I could have been with you longer and, yes, it did end quite quickly. I was more upset at the vet at the clinic for being insensitive." I said this to her and she had tears in her eyes saying, "Yes, the vet at one point was so frustrated that he couldn't fix the situation and that the horse wouldn't get up that he started kicking him." The horse said, "I was upset at the vet but not at you, not ever. I know you felt really helpless and you were just crying and saying stop, and it did get out of hand there for a minute. But then the vet stopped and just said that he was sorry, and left the room saying he needed to cool off and get himself together."

He said again, "No, I'm not mad at you. If there was anything that was a little bit of a problem for me while we were together, it would be that place you were boarding me with all those dogs." My client starts laughing, "Oh, yeah, they had eleven dogs that used to bark all the time." So then he said, "I'm very happy now. I'm living in the south with warm weather and lots of grass and a big field to run in."

Q: Oh, he's reincarnated?

A: Yes, and it was very interesting because I didn't even get this at first. He worded it this way, "I was in the spirit form for a long time, but then my spirit went into a big horse and then I came out a little horse." I repeated, "your spirit went into a big horse and you came out a little horse?" I realized he meant birth, and I had never quite heard it that way. So he was a young horse again and said that he loved her and had no hard feelings whatsoever, and that was it. And she was so relieved, saying, "Oh, thank you so much. What a burden you've lifted from me."

Q: It sounds like many of your clients seem to have a lot of guilt or regret, very difficult emotions to process through after an animal dies, but then much relief when they're able to know that their animal is okay, and even where they are sometimes. A good animal communicator really bridges that communication, and I think that's really important. How can someone find an animal communicator who is of quality?

A: I've worked with Penelope Smith, who is one of the founders of animal communication. She started discovering on her own, and training with the few who were already doing this, and she started teaching. I had been practicing on my own and doing work for about ten years before I went to see her. I recommend her wholeheartedly, either going to her or to somebody else who has trained with her.

Q: *Is there a place people can call for a referral?*

A: Yes. She has a newsletter called *The Species Link* with a listing of animal communicators that she has trained herself, or else they have written documentation of their work. I also know people who have worked with Penelope and then not used their animal communication abilities in the best way. So she uses a code of ethics now, and I recommend the people who are currently connected with her. It's a really good place.

Q: *Is there anything else that you feel is relevant for celebrating the human/animal bond in life and death?*

A: I can answer that by telling you about my companion, Makeba, a large Australian Shepherd/Black Lab mix, who has been one of the most important individuals in my life. She helped me heal after my car accident, and has been totally dedicated to me and completely loving. There were times I was so depressed that I didn't want to even get out of bed, and she would come trotting in saying, "Come on, get up, we're going outside and I'm not going to stop barking until you take me for a walk." And I would tell her to go away, feeling horrible. I didn't want to get up. So she'd go in the other room for about fifteen minutes and then come back in again.

Q: So she really helped rehabilitate you, bring you back into this life?

A: Yes, she did. After I became physically stronger and healthier, she was one of my teachers for the animal communication. She would just stare at me and I just knew she was trying to tell me something, and I'd ask, "What? What? I want to understand you. I really want to know what it is." Then she'd say "Okay, I will accentuate what I want." She'd lead me into the kitchen with her head nodding up to the counter, she would even move her little eyebrows toward food on the counter.

So most of my tests were guessing what kind of food she most wanted from the kitchen. Then I kept practicing that way, thinking she must be saying this or that, and working on hearing that in my mind. And then it became really amazing when I was in the living room one day and I didn't know where she was. I was just sitting there and I heard really clearly in a voice, different than mine, "I need water in my water bowl." I wondered if I really heard this, so I jump up and sure enough, she's in the kitchen standing over her empty water bowl.

Q: *Oh, my goodness. So you knew you really were starting to get it.*

A: Yes, I knew that I was getting stronger and clearer.

Q: *What a gift.*

A: Yes. She really was, and still is, a wonderful helper and protector, this companion of mine.

Blackie

Dhani Mertin-Zovic, age 10

I remember very little but still enough to tell the story about my black fish who was about pinkie-long. Very cheerful. This is how it all started.

One day I saw this beautiful fish in a pet store. I asked my mom if I could have it. She thought about it for awhile. Then she stopped the car, opened the door and said come on.

When we got in the pet shop I walked straight for the fish and asked how much it cost. The clerk said fifty cents, plus the tank and food, pebbles, and a castle should equal about $3.00 + tax. The clerk stopped to think. Oh dear… $3.68. My mom bought it and we went home.

I put him in a bowl and named him Blackie. I played with him for awhile then I took him outside and showed him that we lived on Downer Avenue. For some reason I think he gave me a wink. I smiled back.

Twelve months later it was his birthday. I gave him extra food and attention. I even let him watch an hour and a half of MTV. And the nicest thing was that he got to stay up two hours past his bedtime.

Every time I left for school I missed him a lot. And

every time I came back he would be very happy to see me. The days passed like that until one day, a hot summer afternoon, I came home and he was floating above the water. I took him outside, buried him in dirt and never saw him again.

Blackie was three years old when he died. I still believe that if you listen hard enough you can still hear him swimming in the heavenly waters above.

The End

Misty

Sue Aldene

Part I

"Malagold Misty Melody" was a wonderful Golden Retriever girl. She hated being an obedience or show dog, because her true love was helping to heal the lives of others as a therapy dog. This is the one area in which she excelled. She was the best therapy dog I have seen. She didn't do tricks, she just gave unconditional love to ill patients who needed her. Once, an occupational therapist asked if she could sense the people who didn't like her. My answer was that she thought everyone liked her. Almost everyone did! In the five years we volunteered, she brought smiles to the faces of literally hundreds of mentally ill patients. According to the staff, some patients smiled only when the dogs came to visit.

During one of our visits, we noticed a man who had always been in his own world. He never seemed to care that we were there and really showed no interest in us. He was sitting near some people who were enjoying Misty's company. She went over to him and he ignored her. The therapist who escorted us on our visits placed this gentleman's hands on Misty's head, so he could feel how soft her coat was. Well, he clamped onto her ears tightly. He didn't pull, he just grasped them firmly and looked into her eyes. Most dogs would squirm and try to pull away. Not Misty, she just stayed there, patient as ever! During this time, his vacant stare focused on Misty's face and he smiled. The therapist said that was the first time she had ever seen him smile. Each of our visits after that brought focus to this man's eyes and a smile to his face.

Another time, the therapist who escorted us knocked on the door of a male patient who did not speak English. As she knocked, the door opened a bit. She held the door open just far enough to ask if the man wanted to see the dog. The man did not understand and looked confused. By this time, Misty had begun to wonder what was going on and peered around the door. The man saw Misty and sat up. He then very enthusiastically invited us in. His face lit up and he began to tell a story. He was obviously telling the story of a dog, a dear friend with whom he had shared his heart. He spoke with animation and affection. Since he wasn't speaking English, all I could do was smile and nod. After a few minutes, he was apparently tired of my bobbing head and finished telling the story to Misty. The story ended the way most animal stories end. His speech grew slower and more somber. A few tears fell from his eyes. He gave a kiss and a hug to the only one in the building who understood him, Misty.

She brought so much to so many, and all she ever wanted in return was a stroke on the head and a scratch behind the ears. She taught me about volunteerism and commitment. She was in her element when offering therapy, and only needed me as a chauffeur on those occasions, because she had the program in her heart.

Part II

It was just after our fifth anniversary of volunteering at Mendota Mental Health Institute when Misty and I took some time off. She was having some difficulty with a front leg and was limping on and off. The week off turned into a month off, as the lesion on Misty's foot would erupt and heal and then erupt again. I also changed jobs and was unable to work out a time with my supervisor to go to Mendota. Another month passed, and Misty developed an enlargement in her neck. Surgery and biopsies revealed that Misty's toe was the site of a malignant melanoma, and her neck held a node full of lymphoma. On May 5, 1998, one of Misty's vets, and her favorite vet technician, came to our house. We helped her to the Bridge from our front yard.

But the business of the cancer remained. I was left with veterinary fees for surgery, biopsies, treatments and cremation. Misty was co-owned by my roommate, an employee of the clinic, and therefore her treatments had been billed at a substantial discount. But the terms of the discount depended upon paying the balance in full immediately, which I was unable to do. One day in August, I received a call from the clinic's office manager to discuss options for payment, such as a creditor who offered financing for assorted medical/dental/veterinary debts, so I stopped by the clinic to pick up an application.

About a week later, I received another call from the office manager, and cringed because that application was still sitting on the seat of my car. But she had much different news for me. The night before, an anonymous person had come into the clinic and paid my account in full!! I now understand that "what goes around, comes around." Misty gave so much to strangers that it is fitting that a "stranger" gave back to her.

Misty always led with her heart. She was wonderful and very special, and there will never be another one like her.

Empathy of a Mare

Amy Crane Johnson

Grieving her loss, still-tender
woman slowly mounts my back.
My rounded belly, a reminder,
catches her familiar nudge of heel.

Her loss is my loss
as we ride and we ride.
Rhythm of heart and hoof compliment,
soothe my own quiet load.

Female to female, I sense building
unease, a need to release. We race
on and on through weeping
branches, until her scream
of loss is finally born.

Our nostrils flare
as sides contract,
choking relief conceived
in an afterbirth of tears.

We slowly return, heads bent.
Sweet tears merge with sweat
on shiny flanks. She leans
to pat my swell of unborn foal.

Crossing Over

C.O. Smith

For Max
July 1986 - July 1999

Make medicine from suffering
—Zen Koan

By the time this is finished, he will be
gone – sixty nine pounds of Springer
Spaniel flesh, belly muscle, tooth

and bone gone to dust. Who knows
what finally takes them out, not me,
but the Spirit does move on. I want

to follow this dogchild of mine
the way he's followed me for years, first
crawling in my lap at five weeks old,

there for my grieving of dead
best friends and teachers: Rosie,
Carole and Chuck, then Lynda,

Shirley. And if he's joining them now,
then who's to soothe me? My selfish
cries of wanting only him are a vortex

spinning into grief's deepest bucket.
And now I'm forty-eight hours out
from his last breath, trying to make

sense of why I wasn't with him
when he died, my sharp need
to have him wait for me, that if I

held him – my little moodling doggie –
he'd have less pain just knowing
I was with him all the way. I've fantasized

a million times the way it could
have been, the way it really was,
and each time I circle the drain, screaming

in my rage, my whole body
shuddering down with guilt
and sorrow. And I feel the wound

afresh. There's no escaping it. I want
to die, to cross over, to find my mooka
doodle boy and scoop him up to my chest,

squeeze all my love back into him, as if
he's lost it in his passing. Oh Max.
Please come back. As I sit here holding

his smelly toys, his presence calls
from my deepest core, beating a loud
rhythm, letting me know that this grief is an ocean

plunging the heart of its oxygen. We ride
each wave and undertow as captives,
as unwilling swimmers who must each

take turns breathing, moving, being
perfectly still, so that the other one
won't give out. It is always the same –

first I carry him, then he
carries me. And now only he
can give me the strength
to give him over.

Learning About Love

For My Best Friend, Spike: 1985-1999

Julie Kaufman

Part One:

Oh Spike. How can I speak about all that you have gifted to me? The truth is that I never knew love until you came into my life. You taught me love. Pure, unconditional love and forgiveness. How empty and hollow my life would have been without you. Of that I am certain.

There are so many people and places that have passed through my window of awareness. So many whom I have claimed to love, and those who have professed their love for me. But none compare to the relationship you and I shared over the past fourteen years. Yours was the longest and dearest committed relationship I have ever known. A true friend, the best I have ever had. You were the healthiest relationship I have ever experienced. Humans could learn millenniums of wisdom from who you were, and now who you are in your spirit form. I told my partner today that I loved you more than anything or anyone I have known in my life. Paws down, no question. That's a pretty strong statement about how well you taught me, and you did it without words. Even when my heart was black and filled with rage from destructive patterns of thought, you loved me and you would not leave me. You, Spike, my committed, loyal angel wrapped in fur.

I dreamt about you one night when I was twenty-one. In the dream you said, "Mom, I'm ready to go, come and get me." I could see your sweet, soft puppy fur. Your eyes dark and empathetic. The dream was so powerful that I went straight to the humane society as soon as they opened the next day. I wondered how in the world I would know who you were, but you gave me so many signs. As soon as I walked down the aisle of kennels containing dozens of puppies, there you were – the only puppy who was not barking and playing. Your ears long and curving off in several directions, you looked like Yoda from Star Wars. Then, looking straight up at me, you spoke without sound. "I'm ready." It was an instant bond that will remain with me for the rest of this life and eternity.

Having grown up in and out of foster homes and living with a new family on the average of every six months to two years, my trust levels were not remarkably high. I had learned that bonding was a temporary convenience and that people could not be counted on for long periods. In my adult life, I noticed that when dating or making friends, the strong urge to move on after a period of time mimicked the shifts in my childhood. I had no sense of commitment, love, loyalty or trust because it had not been a part of my upbringing. As a child, my relationships had been based on bonds of sympathetic care-taking, and more a function of duty than love.

Putting the fun in dysfunctional was the theme of my

early years. I knew that people who supposedly loved me might also abuse and violate me. And if you had not come into my life, I would not have had any good examples of love, trust, loyalty and commitment. You were a success with me. I now know how to love others the way that you loved me. For that I can never thank you enough. I follow your lead when establishing friendships and love relationships: Look carefully at who you are dealing with, and once you have a good foundation of character, move forward. Then love with all your heart and soul! Be fair and consistent. Ask for what you want and make your communications clear. Have fun, sleep enough, eat enough, play enough, enjoy and live in each present moment, and forgive as soon as possible after a conflict so that you can have the quality of life you deserve.

It has only been two days since the vet came to the house to euthanize you. Although you could still get up and around, your bowel control had begun to go awry six months ago, and that day your bladder gave out as well. I asked you if you were ready to go. You quietly replied with a clear "Yes." You had held together over the past year, more for me than for yourself, and now it was time for me to love you enough to let you go. It was the right thing to do. It was also one of the hardest things I have ever done.

I made you a big steak, the first in a year since you had been on a special diet. I took you and the puppy for a last walk down the nature trail near our house where you had walked every morning with me for so many years. This was the first time you made it all the way to the trail in a year. We rested in the grass for awhile until you were able to make the trip home.

Many of your friends came over to say good bye to you and it was extremely bittersweet. I'm glad in retrospect that they had a chance to do so, but it was so hard.

Finally, when many who loved you had said their good-byes, I had a chance to be alone with you and tell you how deeply I loved you. I told you it was OK to go, that I would find a way to live without your physical presence in my life. I told you how much you had taught me and what a good boy you were. I said I would always love you and remember the things you had taught me. I asked your spirit guides and angels to help us both through your crossing over, that it would be easy and peaceful. The only way I could get through this was to keep my mind focused on what was best for you and away from my deep searing pain over losing you.

Dr. Tom came to the door and you jumped up to greet him, happy as always to have a friend visit. I thought it was good that I didn't wait to make this decision until you were so bad that you couldn't get up at all. Then you came and laid down on the blanket I bought for your final resting spot. I helped Dr. Tom give you the injection that gave you peace and rest. I held you and stroked your ears because you always loved that so much. I told you what a good boy you were and how much I loved you. It was over and there was a sense of peace in the room. We all cried and thought of how much we loved you. You were the best friend this girl ever had. Your presence in my life made me a much better human being than I would have ever dreamed.

I no longer fear death. I will look forward to our reunion. Until that time, I will visualize you running in green fields filled with grass and flowers with all of your beloved friends like Chelsea, Bear, and others who are with you in Dog Heaven. I will continue to dedicate my life to improving the quality of life for both humans and animals. Perhaps I can share a fraction of the love you showered upon me over the fourteen years we shared on this earth.

Part Two:

Messenger from the Spiritual Realm

Approximately a week and a half after Spike died, I had a strange experience that both startled me and offered me a deep sense of peace.

Late one evening, I was suddenly overwhelmed by the smell of a strong, sweet perfume. It was, in fact, so strong that it was nauseating and gave me a headache. I asked my girlfriend what she was wearing because she smelled like a siren, a lady of the night. She replied that she was not wearing any perfume, but that she was experiencing a different smell that was quite loud, the smell of dog. I wondered why we could be smelling such different strong odors, and then dismissed the issue.

The next day while typing on the computer in the living room, this time alone in the house, I was again overwhelmed by the same strong, nauseating scent of perfume. I angrily got up to go and find out what soap or lotion was annoying me, and walked briskly down the hall to the bathroom. After a thorough search of the soaps and lotions in the drawers, I found none that emitted such a smell. Irritated by not finding the source of the smell, I sat back down on the couch and quietly realized that the odor was not from a physical source. A strong inner voice cued me that this was a signal from the spiritual realm. Someone was trying to get my attention. They were not being subtle at this point. It was becoming obvious that the smell was not intended to be ignored.

Over the next few minutes, I stopped my typing and intentionally got more relaxed and quiet. I became aware of the presence of a woman. She was in her eighties, businesslike, with short red hair. She was dressed in a white suit and appeared as a slightly translucent figure in the living room which was filled with bright morning sun. The hair on the back of my neck stood on end. The figure spoke to me and said "I will take care of Spike for you." At that point, Spike appeared and sat at her side. He looked young and vigorous, and yet calm. He was also a translucent version of his old physical self. I then wondered if the woman was a relative or friend who had died. She responded to my thought by saying that she was not. She was there to help and again affirmed that she would take good care of Spike for me. Then she turned and walked through and out of the room accompanied by a happy, healthy spirit Spike. As soon as they departed, so did the strong perfume.

I was overwhelmed with a sense of peace and have been much more at ease with Spike's death since the communication. In spite of this reassurance of his spiritual well-being, I do miss him every day and cry often. I feel that the tears are more for my own loss and the grief of missing that daily unconditional love he so faithfully offered. I know in my heart that he is out of pain and in good hands.

Even though I consider myself sensitive and aware of spiritual realities, it took some effort to become quiet and listen to hear the message. I am grateful for the opportunity to have become aware of the messenger, and for her efforts to console me.

Chapter Five

It is helpful to quiet the mind by practicing a basic meditation before doing the exercises. The suggested Relaxed Breathing and Tension Release techniques can be found in the front of the book in the Introduction.

What can you do to mark and celebrate the momory of your loved one? Plant a tree? Write a poem? Do whatever you feel led to do in order to translate feelings into actions. If it's hard to decide, become still and ask the spirit of your pet: "What can I do to honor the love I have for you, my friend for eternity? I am listening closely. What are you sharing from the spirit realm?

When you have done what you feel led to do, be sure and return to it whenever you feel lonesome for your animal. It will always be there for you as a tangible, soothing connection to this very important relationship you shared.

Resources

The IAMS Pet Loss Support Resource Center: 1-800-332-7738

Recommended Reading

Angel Catcher: A Journal of Loss and Remembrance by Kathy and Amy Eldon. 1998. Chronicle Books, ISBN: 0-8118-1731-8.

Cold Noses at the Pearly Gates by Gary Kurz. 1997. ISBN: 0966611705.

Coping With Sorrow by Moira K. Anderson. 1996 Alpine Publications, ISBN: 0931866979.

Coping With The Loss Of A Pet: A Gentle Guide For All Who Love A Pet Christina M. Lemieux, Ph.D. 1988, Wallace R. Clark, Reading, PA. ISBN: 0-9622158-0-5.

Dog Heaven by Cynthia Rylant (Illustrator). 1995, Scholastic Trade. ISBN: 0-590417010. Website: www.dogheaven.com.

Forever Friends: Resolving Grief After The Loss Of A Beloved Animal by Joan Coleman. 1993, J.C. Tara Enterprises, Inc., Las Vegas, NV. ISBN: 1-883018-03-X.

On Death and Dying by Elizabeth Kubler-Ross. Reprinted 1997, Simon & Schuster. ISBN: 0684842238.

Pet Loss: A Spiritual Guide by Eleanor L. Harris. 1997, Llewellyn Publications. ISBN: 1567183476.

The Loss of a Pet: A Guide To Coping With The Grieving Process When A Pet Dies by Wallace Sife, Ph.D. 1998, Howell Book House, New York, NY. ISBN: 0-87605-197-2. Website: www.mgr.com.

Many of these books can be reviewed and purchased at www.amazon.com.

Recommended Web Sites

The following web sites are good sources for information and support, and have valuable links to other pet loss web sites.

www.katsden.com

www.petloss.com

www.petsforum.com (The Delta Society Website: actually Randy's Fishroom, a cool site about animal/human bond)

www.homevet.com

www.dogheaven.com

www.olywa.net

www.mgr.com

Contributors' Notes

Kathy Agenten

I wrote this piece to help other animal lovers with the loss of a very dear friend and the end of a special relationship. It does hurt, but with time, understanding and love of family and other animals, the hurt passes, the wonderful memories remain. I have always had animals in my life. What a true blessing. I currently board horses for my employment. Our family has raised and shown horses for over twenty-five years. Animals have absolutely filled my life with joy and comfort. I have so many priceless riches, a wonderful family, true friends and exceptional animal companions.

Susan Aldene

Susan Aldene began working with dogs in 1986 for a handler/Golden breeder who also had a boarding kennel. Misty was then about eight weeks old, and they bonded quickly. She was introduced to conformation and obedience competition while working at the kennel, and continued to pursue other dog sports when she left.

Now, thirteen years later, she is an agility instructor and exhibitor, who also enjoys taking action photos of dogs in agility competitions. Her newest canine project is a Beagle puppy who is being shown in conformation and training in agility, tracking and obedience.

Richard J. Binder

Richard J. Binder lives in Milwaukee, Wisconsin, and works for a local environment and engineering consulting firm. He likes to spend time hiking with his faithful dog, Max, a ten-year-old yellow Labrador Retriever.

Laura Borman

After Kate's death I got my Annie Lochleven Annet of Aberdeen, and on January 8, 1999, Annie and I adopted Diablo from a Collie rescue. He had been through four foster families in one month and was terribly fearful and traumatized. He didn't even want to get in the car when we came to take him to his new home. He is quickly coming out of his shell though, and has rapidly become a valued family member. It is wonderful to watch him break through his fears and explore new aspects of his environment.

I have always had a strong connection to animals. They communicate their thoughts and feelings with incredible clarity, and the idea that animals have no feelings or thought process seems alien and silly to me. One of the many gifts that animals bring to us is their ability to compel us to broaden our own perspective.

Sue Daubner

Born in Germany and raised in Norway until the age of five, Sue Daubner grew up in Chicago. She remembers taking her swimming lesson money and sneaking out to ride horses. Mother to Maia Michalsen (*Frewin, My Free and Noble Friend*), she currently lives with her husband in Door County where they own and operate Solbjorg's Gift Shop and the Sister Bay Cafe.

Karen Dustman

Karen Dustman is a freelance writer and author of two nonfiction books. She has written extensively about the human-animal bond and animal holistic health. Her work includes over 100 articles on animal related subjects for popular magazines such as *Natural Pet*, *Vegetarian Times* and *Ladies Home Journal*. She lives in the mountains of central California with her husband and Macaw and African Grey Parrot. Both birds are a robust nineteen years of age. Karen followed her passion, giving up a prosperous career in law to devote her time to educating the public about animal related topics.

Kathy E. Esch

Kathy E. Esch was born in Madison, WI with the talent to draw and the love of animals. After spending 1977 in the San Francisco Bay area researching artistic styles, Kathy returned to Madison to attend Madison Area Technical College. There she earned an Associate Degree in Commercial Art, majoring in photography and drawing. Now working in the commercial art field, she attended the University of Wisconsin, Madison in the Fine Arts Department.

"Pet Portraiture is now my main focus. My goal is to create an anatomically correct portrait that communicates the unconditional bond between and dog and its owner. Or that distinctive characteristic of one's cat, be it a comic or a regal queen."

Dr. Heather Evans

Dr. Heather Evans received her doctorate in veterinary medicine from the University of Tennessee College of Veterinary Medicine in 1994. Soon after graduation, she discovered her interest in alternative medicine and pursued certification in animal acupuncture and chiropractic. She recently established her small animal practice in Minneapolis, Minnesota, offering acupuncture, chiropractic, nutritional counseling and herbal therapy for her feline and canine friends. Dr. Heather shares her home with her dog, Zac, and her two cats, Sidney and Abraham.

Sue Heilberger

Sue Heilberger lives in Whitefish Bay, Wisconsin, with her husband, Ross, and daughter, Abby. They have recently adopted a Golden Retriever puppy named Becky, after Bruiser's mother. Sue is a registered nurse and teaches nursing at Concordia University.

Mickey Hopper

Mickey is a full time dressage trainer in Lancaster, CA. She owns Sweetwater Ranch, where thirty horses board. She shares her life with fiancé and poet Robert Keeler, and seven dogs, three barn cats, her Thoroughbred stallion, Alissando, Robert's Arabian mare, and three brood mare/lesson horses.

"I Lay You Down To Rest" was written as a parting tribute to Apollo, a thirty-four-year-old Palomino gelding. It expresses the feelings of sorrow, duty and remembrance that spring forth when we make the decision to put an old friend down. Horses are the most gentle and patient spirits on the planet earth, and they have many lessons to teach us. All they ask of us is that we slow down and listen to them.

Amy Crane Johnson

Amy is a copywriter for the advertising agency, Raven Tree Arts, in De Pere, Wisconsin. This agency is home to six birds who have free flight through part of the office. At home Amy is mother to two children, a husband and a Lhasa Apso named Walker.

Elizabeth Johnson

Elizabeth (Betsy) is currently pursuing a photography degree at MATC. At the time she wrote the haiku, "Picture of Cat," she was ten years old. She still has the cat picture, but more importantly, she still loves cats and animals of all kinds.

Dr. Julie Kaufman

Julie Kaufman lives with a Boxer named "Evander," two cats "Nikolai" and "Natasha," two canaries, two finches and her pregnant mare "Pasha."

Dr. Kaufman is a Doctor of Chiropractic and a Certified Animal Chiropractor. She graduated from Cleveland Chiropractic College in 1989, and has worked for the past ten years on large and small animals throughout Wisconsin. She was a senior instructor and board member for the American Veterinary Chiropractic Association from 1989-1993, where she currently guest lectures. She earned the second Animal Chiropractic Certification awarded in the world; there are now approximately 600 certified animal chiropractors worldwide.

Dr. Kaufman founded the Wisconsin Professional Animal Chiropractor's Association, WIPACA, and developed the holistic equine education program, Equinox, for horse owners, professionals and trainers.

Recent articles include: "Animal Chiropractic, Realigning the Human-Animal Bond," *The Holistic Health Journal*, Sept. 1997, and "Equine Alternative Therapy: Chiropractic Care," *The Sentinel*, by Carol Perkins, (Libertyville IL), Vol. 24, No. 4, July 1996.

Dr. Kaufman has been interviewed on CNN, and on the nationally syndicated radio show, *Here's To Your Health*. She has also been interviewed for *Equus Magazine*, *Natural Pet Magazine*, *Farm Show Magazine*, and *Doris Day's Animal Guardian Magazine*.

She currently lectures throughout the country to horse and dog clubs, veterinary schools, and holistic groups. Dr. Kaufman is committed to communication and actions that enhance the quality of life for animals and nurture the human-animal bond.

Terry LaMantia

Terry is a glass artist, who lives in Hartland, Wisconsin, with her husband Joe, son Doug, and cat Fred. Fred misses Brownie and his sister Ginger who passed away last fall, but at age twenty, he has expressed a desire to live out his golden years without breaking in a new kitten or puppy.

Bobbi Mallace

I cannot imagine living without dogs because I am constantly learning from them. My husband and I currently own rare breeds but have owned many mixed breed dogs. I have written a regular column for a national breed club newsletter, and my occupations include figure skating coach, bareback trick horse riding, and sculpting in stone, as well as story writing.

Adrienne Martin

Adrienne Martin recalls a story her mother recited many times throughout Adrienne's childhood. The incident occurred when they lived in Boston and would influence her and create a special bond throughout her life. Adrienne, two years old, ran out onto a busy road while playing. Topper, the family Collie, ran out after her and saved her life by physically knocking her out of harm's way.

Hearing her mother speak lovingly of Topper's courage, Adrienne realized that animals have a sense of intuitive knowing beyond normal senses, and that both animals and humans have access to that energy that is available for universal mind. Adrienne now lives in southern Wisconsin and uses her clairsensient abilities for the benefit of animals and humans.

Dhani Mertin-Zovic

I am ten years old and very athletic. I play baseball, basketball, football, tennis and ping pong. I like collecting bird feathers, autographs and drumsticks. I have a six-year-old Golden Retriever named Risty, who is fourty-two in human years. I have had three other animals, including Blackie, the fish. Josey and Kristy were two great Goldens who lived with us. I knew them since I was a baby. They were put to sleep at ages ten and twelve respectively because of having cancer.

I hope my piece will help heal others by reaching out to them and saying "it's okay." If you think hard enough, you can still see your beloved but lost pet, no matter what kind of pet.

Maia Michalsen

I live in Kentucky and am an equine/human massage

therapist and Reiki master. My bond with animals has always been strong and has taught and guided me down a great healing journey. I own an Thoroughbred gelding named Mr. Bubbles, who was a troubled soul. My shadow is Moose, a Jack Russell, who is here to watch over me and show people that there are mellow, sweet Jacks out there. He is my little Buddha.

I am honored to have a piece in this book and hope it helps others understand they aren't alone in their grief and loss. We must celebrate the wonderful bond we have with our animal friends.

Dr. Dawn Mogilevisky

Dr. Dawn Mogilevisky has practiced veterinary medicine in Wisconsin for the past nine years. She specializes in small animal conventional medicine, surgery and holistic care including acupuncture. She lives with her husband, two sons and their two cats. Dr. Dawn had published several articles pertaining to breast cancer research prior to becoming a doctor of veterinary medicine.

C.O. Smith

C.O. Smith is a freelance writer and home healthcare worker who misses her little moodlyboy Max. She is grateful for their long life together, from July 1987 to July 1999, and is continuing *Max & Friends*, a pet sitting, walking, and taxi service, in memory of him.

Carmen Rasmussen

Carmen Rasmussen lives in southern Wisconsin with her husband, son and two Scottish Deerhounds, *Dirk* and *Caelin*. They have had Deerhounds for the past ten years and belong to the National Scottish Deerhound Club, which is their major social interest. Carmen has been involved in teaching puppy classes for the past several years.

Margaret Rowland

Margaret is keenly interested in alternative forms of medicine and medical treatment for both humans and animals. She is dedicated to pets, and is a true believer in the God-given love they offer. She holds a B.A. in English, an M.A., is working on her Ph.D. at the University of Wisconsin Madison, and has completed programs in both Reiki and massage.

Cheryl Sheehan

I am a studio artist with two Great Danes (one of whom thinks she's a human), and three cats (one of whom thinks she is a dog).

Companion animals have always been an integral part of my life, nurturing me with their devotion as well as inspiring much of my art work. They are my touchstones – reminding me to be joyful, showing me how to live in the moment and offering me the gift of deep and unconditional love.

The poem included in this book was written after I lost a particularly sweet Great Dane who had been part of my life for much too short a time. He was one of those emotionally gifted animals whom we rarely encounter in our lives unless we are very lucky or very needy. He was a gem. His name was Merlyn, and I know he continues to exist – the signs have been unmistakable. Our bond remains unbroken.

Synthia Smith

Sindy has owned Irish Setter dogs for over twenty-nine years. She reports having become smitten at first sight. She currently lives with her Irish Setters Diana and Sarah, and her squirrel Zoe, who is Sindy's second rehabilitation squirrel that decided to make a permanent home with Sindy. She has worked as a veterinary technician and loves to share her animal experiences to help others. Sindy also lives with five sugar gliders: Angel, Arrow, Angelique, Aeriel and Airianna.

Asia Voight

As a child, I had a deep spiritual connection to animals. Often they would communicate to me with images and words. A fiery car accident eleven years ago changed my life. This near-death experience left me with a partial hearing loss, but it spiritually reawakened the perceptions and unique listening abilities I had as a child, thus, happily restoring my connection to the animals.

I studied with Penelope Smith, a world famous animal communicator and author, and then began practicing professionally, helping people and their animal companions deepen their relationships. This work has really been a joy for me.

I currently live with my partner on a small farm in rural Stoughton, Wisconsin, with our family, two dogs, seven cats and two horses.

Barbara Walsh

I am a Master's prepared Clinical Nurse Specialist who works with individuals who have wounds, ostomies and incontinence. My previous publications have been in professional journals, most recently *Multidisciplinary Management of Altered Body Image in the Patient with an Ostomy.*

Loving and being loved by three cats, Cissy, Megan and Caity, has enriched my life in untold ways. I can no longer imagine my life without a cat to share it with. My hope is that my story will help others realize that you can grow and move on from the death of a "best friend" and that all the joy and love far outweighs the pain. Keep your heart open; there is a lot of love out there just waiting for you.